Listening to

Rural Midwestern Idioms/ Folk Sayings

A Lively and Entertaining Guide to Rural Midwestern Idioms/Folk Sayings

by Bob Bohlken

All inquiries should be addressed to the publisher at:

Images Unlimited Publishing
P.O. Box 305
Maryville, MO 64468
info@imagesunlimitedpublishing.com
http://www.imagesunlimitedpublishing.com

Interior art: Bobby Gumm
Cover and interior design: Teresa Carter
Cover picture: Mike Steiner/Nodaway County Historical Society

ISBN 978-0-930643-34-8
Second Edition

Printed in the United States of America

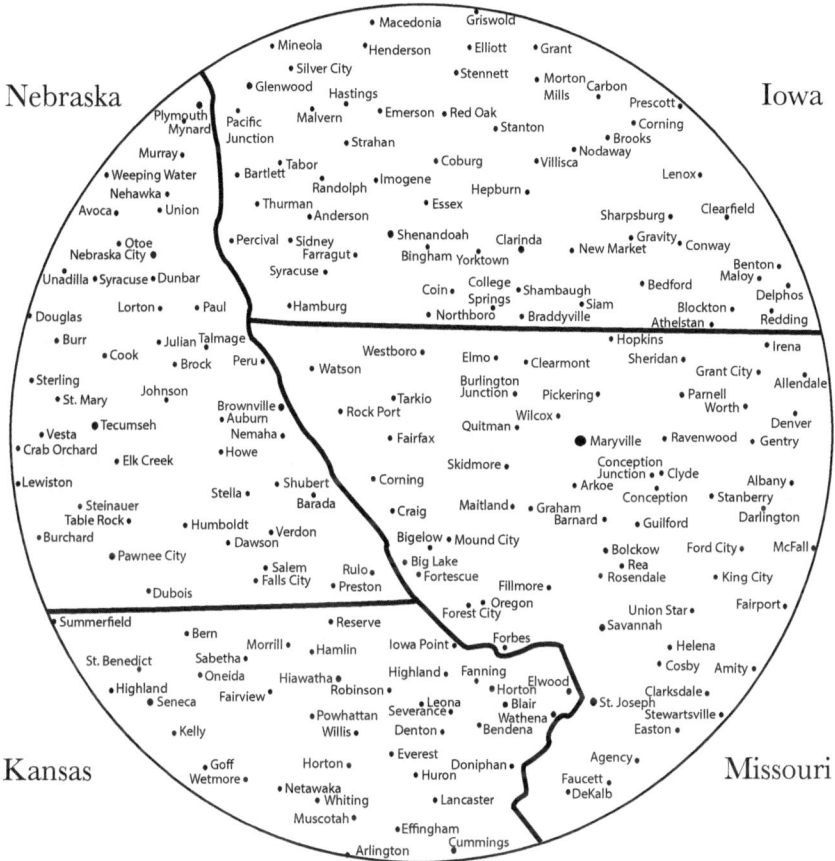

Nebraska

Iowa

Kansas

Missouri

Macedonia • • Griswold
• Mineola • Henderson • Elliott • Grant
• Silver City • Stennett • Morton Carbon
• Glenwood Hastings Mills
Plymouth Pacific Malvern • Emerson • Red Oak Prescott •
Mynard Junction • Stanton • Corning
Murray • • Strahan • Brooks
• Weeping Water • Tabor • Coburg • Villisca • Nodaway
Nehawka • • Bartlett Randolph • Imogene Hepburn • Lenox •
Avoca • • Union • Thurman • Essex
• Anderson Sharpsburg • Clearfield
• Otoe • Percival • Sidney • Shenandoah Clarinda • Gravity • Conway
Nebraska City • Farragut Bingham Yorktown • New Market Benton •
Unadilla • Syracuse • Dunbar Syracuse • Maloy •
Coin • College • Shambaugh • Bedford Delphos
Douglas Lorton • • Paul • Hamburg Springs • Siam Blockton • Redding
• Burr • Julian Talmage • Northboro • Braddyville Athelstan •
• Cook • Brock Peru • Westboro • Elmo • • Clearmont • Hopkins • Irena
• Sterling • Watson Sheridan • Grant City •
• St. Mary Johnson Burlington Pickering • Parnell Allendale
• Vesta • Tecumseh Brownville • • Tarkio Junction • Wilcox • Worth • Denver
• Crab Orchard Nemaha • • Rock Port Quitman • • Maryville • Ravenwood • Gentry
• Elk Creek • Howe • Fairfax Conception
Lewiston • • Shubert • Corning Skidmore • Junction • • Clyde Albany •
• Steinauer Stella • Barada • Craig Maitland • • Graham • Arkoe Conception • Stanberry
Table Rock • • Humboldt • Verdon Bigelow • Mound City Barnard • • Guilford Darlington
• Burchard • Dawson • Big Lake • Bolckow Ford City • McFall
• Pawnee City • Salem Rulo • Fillmore • • Rea • King City
• Falls City • Preston • Fortescue • Oregon • Rosendale
• Dubois Forest City Union Star • Fairport •
Summerfield • • Reserve • Savannah
• Bern Morrill • Iowa Point • Forbes • Helena
St. Benedict Sabetha • • Hamlin Highland • Fanning • Cosby Amity •
• Highland • Oneida Hiawatha • Robinson • • Horton Elwood Clarksdale •
• Seneca Fairview • • Leona • Blair • St. Joseph Stewartsville •
• Powhattan Severance • Wathena Easton •
• Kelly Willis • Denton • • Bendena
• Everest Agency •
• Goff Horton • • Huron Doniphan • Faucett •
Wetmore • • Netawaka • Lancaster • DeKalb
• Whiting
Muscotah • • Effingham
• Arlington Cummings

Dedication

To the hundreds of Rural Midwestern Folk who have
contributed to this collection and to my understanding
of the rural midwestern culture of the past.

Acknowledgements

Special thanks to my spouse and assistant in this endeavor, Mary Riley Bohlken, to Kay Wilson, publisher of the **Nodaway News Leader** and to Lee Jackson, publisher of Images Unlimited.

Thanks to selected members of the International Listening Association, the Missouri Folklore Society, Missouri Writers Guild, Nodaway County Historical Society, Maryville Optimist Club, Men's Forum of Maryville, Host Lion's Club of Maryville, Rotary International Club, American Legion Post 100, Conception Abbey and St. Gregory's Parish.

Thanks to selected residents of Palm Resaca Mobile Park, Brownsville, Texas, Nemaha County Good Samaritan Center, Auburn, Neb.; Nodaway Nursing Home, Parkdale Manor Care Center and Maryville Health Care Center all of Maryville, Mo.

Thanks to selected citizens of rural Maryville, Albany, Bethany, Savannah, Parnell, Skidmore, St. Joseph, Fillmore, Pickering, Ravenwood, Rock Port, Hopkins, Craig, Clyde, Conception Junction, Graham, Fairfax, Burlington Junction, Barnard, Mound City and Tarkio, Mo.; Talmage, Peru, Auburn, Nebraska City, Dawson, Verdon, Falls City, Lincoln, Tecumseh, Beatrice, Brock, Cook and Brownville, Neb.; Stanton, Red Oak, Shenandoah, Bedford, Clarinda, Hamburg, Sidney and Winterset, Iowa; and Atchison, Leavenworth and Lawrence, Kan.

Thanks to the selected friends and relatives of the Jacob and Theresa Bohlken and Dan C. Riley Families.

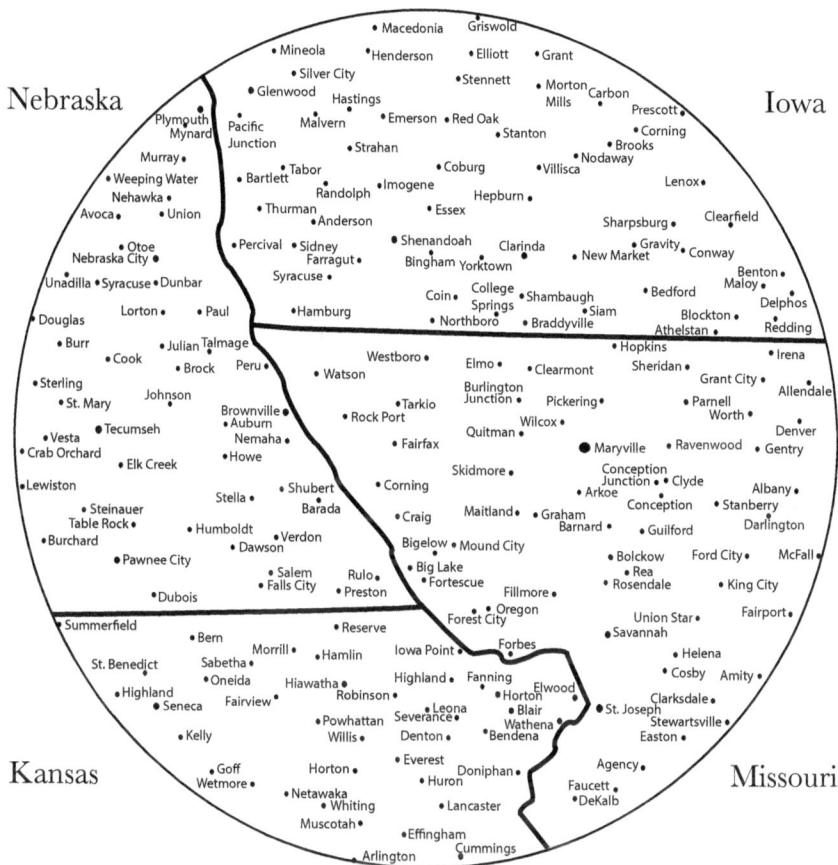

Dedication

To the hundreds of Rural Midwestern Folk who have
contributed to this collection and to my understanding
of the rural midwestern culture of the past.

Acknowledgements

Special thanks to my spouse and assistant in this endeavor, Mary Riley Bohlken, to Kay Wilson, publisher of the **Nodaway News Leader** and to Lee Jackson, publisher of Images Unlimited.

Thanks to selected members of the International Listening Association, the Missouri Folklore Society, Missouri Writers Guild, Nodaway County Historical Society, Maryville Optimist Club, Men's Forum of Maryville, Host Lion's Club of Maryville, Rotary International Club, American Legion Post 100, Conception Abbey and St. Gregory's Parish.

Thanks to selected residents of Palm Resaca Mobile Park, Brownsville, Texas, Nemaha County Good Samaritan Center, Auburn, Neb.; Nodaway Nursing Home, Parkdale Manor Care Center and Maryville Health Care Center all of Maryville, Mo.

Thanks to selected citizens of rural Maryville, Albany, Bethany, Savannah, Parnell, Skidmore, St. Joseph, Fillmore, Pickering, Ravenwood, Rock Port, Hopkins, Craig, Clyde, Conception Junction, Graham, Fairfax, Burlington Junction, Barnard, Mound City and Tarkio, Mo.; Talmage, Peru, Auburn, Nebraska City, Dawson, Verdon, Falls City, Lincoln, Tecumseh, Beatrice, Brock, Cook and Brownville, Neb.; Stanton, Red Oak, Shenandoah, Bedford, Clarinda, Hamburg, Sidney and Winterset, Iowa; and Atchison, Leavenworth and Lawrence, Kan.

Thanks to the selected friends and relatives of the Jacob and Theresa Bohlken and Dan C. Riley Families.

Preface

This book has two purposes: (1) to record the meaning and referent of the rural folk sayings (idioms of the past) of northwest Missouri and surrounding area, and (2) to provide entertainment for those who read and relate to the folk sayings. It is about word phrases that reflect the events, objects, experiences and lives of the farm folks of the past. Many of these are no longer commonplace, as they have faded with time and developing technology. No longer commonplace are the threshing machines, horse and buggy, field corncobs, chamber pots, headcheese, sheep casings, steam engines, molasses, hog butchering, rendering lard, wood/cob sheds, bib and tucker, kit and caboodle, culled chickens, flocks of farm chickens, egg sucking dogs and fox, yard dogs, cream separators, butter churns, printing press, hay stacks and hundreds of others.

In this book the word phrase (the idiom) is explained as an allusion or the basis for indirect suggestion that describes a different circumstance, object or event. Thus, when you read "alludes to" the primary phrase describing the original experience is explained. "Refers to" takes the word phrase and gives it new meaning by associating it with a different experience through the power of verbal suggestion. In order to get meaning from these folk sayings or idioms of the past, one must have concepts of the primary experience as well as the associated experience. For example, I say, "Joe is a chicken." You know that Joe can't literally be a chicken, but you take the characteristics of your concepts of both "Joe" and a "chicken" and associate them mentally. The idiom's meaning is found in the phrase associated with both the original and the suggested concepts, the experiences and the mental processing of the associations. This process of association is called a metaphor, and it is the basis of language.

In order for our language to be interesting, the word concepts need to appeal to the senses and excite the imagination. For example the concept of "death" is abstract, general and complete; whereas, if one says, "crossed the vale (valley)" or "entered into eternal peace" or "passed into God's hands" our minds create tangible images that appeal to the sense of sight and excite imagination. These appeals to the senses and the excitement of the imagination are classified as figures of speech, but they are natural and not intentionally created by the originators of the idioms. The corresponding of accented vowels within the word phrase, the repetition of the same initial word's sound and the sounds of words representing natural sounds all appeal to the senses. "The buzzing bees," "the croaking frogs, "the ticking of the clock," "the mooing of the contended cow" or "the bellering of the sick cow," "pinch a penny," "dime a dozen" all appeal to the senses. The suggestive wording and over exaggeration excite the imagination: "Do what you want in the buggy but don't startle the horses." "A gnat's ass sewed up with a log chain."

One of the difficulties in preserving rural idioms for a geographical region is trying to determine their particular usage in that region known as its isogloss. We are such a transit society that an idiom used here may also be used in rural communities found in other geographical areas. So, a folk saying used here may also have been common in other regions of the country.

Another difficulty is choosing between authenticity and literary taste. Some of the colloquial expression may be classified "unfit for the public reading" because they are crass, crude, uncouth, gross, obscene, repulsive, loathsome and tasteless. I have chosen to favor authenticity over taste and have not used euphemisms. For example I write the authentic saying, "He squeezes a nickel so tight that the buffalo farts" instead of the less vulgar "He squeezes the nickel so tight that the buffalo experiences flatulence."

Another problem is in determining the origin of the idiom. For example take the idiom "kicked the bucket." Some contend that it alludes to the kicking of the bucket out from under the person in the process of hanging him/her. My sources say it comes from the concept of a farmer milking his cow and the farmer kicks the bucket as he falls off the stool and begins the dying process. Some say that "watch your 'p's and 'q's" alludes to keeping track of the number of pints and quarts of beer one drinks in an inn's tavern. My sources say it alludes to the old printing press where the two were easily confused. The origin of the idioms is first a family or community matter and grows from there. For example "Don't mix your meat with your potatoes" and its reference are local, and in my research I did not find its usage elsewhere.

The Author's Perspective of the Compilation Presented in the Midwest Vernacular

This compilation of middle Midwest U.S. folk sayings (idioms) has been "a long row to hoe." We don't claim that it is "the whole piece of cloth;" in fact, it might have just unearthed the "tip of the boulder." Life experiences have played an important part in this compilation for I believe that one should "bloom where one is planted." At the age of 80, I'm "no spring chicken" and I've lived in "this neck of the woods" since birth.

I was born and "reared" in the "jerkwater town" (refers to small towns where the trains only stop long enough to take on water for the steam engines), Talmage Nebraska, just a "hawk and a spit" from Maryville Missouri, the "hub" of this compilation. I was "fetched up" and graduated from Talmage High School in the top ten of the 1953 class. There were ten in the class, and I was one of them. When I was "knee high to a grasshopper," I worked in a hardware store and soon learned that a chamber pot might be called a "thunder mug" or a "slop jar." A "blow hard" who "wore the hat but didn't have the cattle," "nailed me to the wall" while I was trying to "figure out" what he wanted to purchase. I retreated to the back room "with my tail between my legs."

When I was in high school, I worked at the Talmage Hatchery/Produce Store. Here I learned that you "shouldn't count your chickens before they hatch" and that "cream always rises." Being a "half baked" kid, I had to "watch my p's and q's" in testing cream, so as not to get myself "in a pickle." Often during "open night," I would "sit around" listening to the farmers who had come to town in their "best bib and tucker." They "chewed the rag," "shot the breeze" and "spun a few yarns" about the olden days.

Some were "full of prunes," some didn't know "sic cum from com mere," some were "quick as a fox," some had been "bending their elbows" and were "three sheets in the wind" and wanted to "coon wrestle." After I served three years in the U.S Army "ground pounders" during the Korean Conflict, I returned to "this neck of the woods" to attend Peru State College in Nebraska, "down the road a piece" from Talmage. I "burned the midnight oil" studying how to teach speaking, writing, listening and reading. While at college, I "got hitched" to Mary Riley who came from the "jerkwater town" of Dawson, Nebraska, a short distance "as the crow flies" from Maryville, Peru, and Talmage. We "tied the knot" in September 1958. We really "didn't have a pot to pee in" and Mary's mother told her that she "just as well buy herself a washboard and a mirror, so she could watch herself starve to death."

In 1959, I graduated, Mary swallowed a "watermelon seed," I taught language arts and skills at Stanton Iowa, and in August our daughter, Katy, was "brought into the world." The next year, "we pulled up our stakes" and moved to Nebraska City where I taught English language skills, and I also attended the University of Nebraska at Lincoln. Mary "swallowed another watermelon seed" and in June 1962, our son, Dan, "saw the light of day" for the first time. With my master's degree "in hand," we moved back to Peru State College where I became an instructor of language arts and skills in 1963. While "stomping out literary ignorance" at Peru State during the fall and winter semesters, in the summers, I "journeyed" to the University of Kansas in Lawrence seeking a Doctorate in Philosophy. There were some "mud roads," some "bumpy roads," some "roads with a lot of bends," and some times it seemed as if the professors were trying "to make a silk purse out of a sow's ear." In 1969, I "got" the doctorate degree, and in 1970, we "packed our whole kit and caboodle" and moved to Maryville, Missouri, where I "became" the "chair" of the speech and theatre department. In 1979, I "became the "head" of the division of communications. After having a "rhubarb" with the vice president, I "gave up" my administrative responsibilities "that had shortened my stake rope" to become a "full time professor" in 1984. This is when I formally began my study of listening to how people of different localities and vocations used the spoken English language and began gathering a "nest egg" of folk sayings.

Since the year, 2000, when I "went out to pasture," I formally have been collecting folk sayings (idioms) of "rural folks" in this geographical region. I may be "walking on egg shells," but I think that what we "got here is a perty darn good representation," "without beating a dead horse," of the "talk around here in the olden days." I hope you "get a kick out of" reading it and I won't end up "with egg on my face."

A Sampling of Middle Midwestern Folk Sayings (Idioms)

"A large piece of the cloth"

TABLE OF CONTENTS

Appearance

Ugly as a molting hen — alludes to a chicken hen that is losing her feathers, especially around the rear end. Refers to someone who is not clean or neat. *"After she finished the race, she was as ugly as a molting hen."*

Ugly as homemade soap — alludes to soap that is made with tallow and lye and has a dirty yellow color. Refers to someone whose complexion is washed out and unattractive. *"That woman is as ugly as homemade soap."*

Ugly as a mud hen — alludes to a small brownish gray duck. Refers to someone who has unappealing color and shape. *"I don't see what he sees in her; she's as ugly as a mud hen."*

Been hit with an ugly stick — alludes to a person being hit on the face by a stick. Refers to someone who is very, very unattractive. *"Poor Sue must have been hit with the ugly stick."*

Run of the mill — alludes to the production of a very common fabric. Refers to someone or something that is plain and not attractive. *"He has a run of the mill girlfriend."*

Unkempt as a mangy dog — alludes to a dog that suffers from hair and skin disorders created by an infestation of fleas and mites. Refers to someone who lacks grooming and appears dirty. *"After a day in the hay field, he looks unkempt as a mangy dog."*

Ugly enough to gag a maggot — alludes to fly larva that feeds off dead flesh. Refers to someone or something that is really unappealing in looks. *"That horse is ugly enough to gag a maggot."*

Ugly enough to knock a maggot off a gut wagon — alludes to fly larva gathered on a tankage wagon hauling dead animal carcasses to a rendering plant. Refers to someone or something that is really unpleasant or unsightly. *"His old gray mare was ugly enough to knock a maggot off a gut wagon."*

Clean as a hound's tooth — alludes to a dog that chews on bones that clean its teeth. Refers to someone or something that is very clean. *"She keeps herself clean as a hound's tooth."*

Been rode hard and put away wet — alludes to a horse that has been raced hard and not given time to cool down. Refers to someone whose hair, complexion and clothing are in disarray. *"That poor woman looks like she's been rode hard and put away wet."*

Looks like a gnat's ass sewed up with a log chain — alludes to the rear end of a very small flying insect and a very large chain. It is an impossible exaggeration. It refers to a task or sewing that appears very poorly done. *"Her mending of his shirt looks like a gnat's ass sewed up with a log chain."*

Too big for his britches — alludes to very tight or short trousers. Refers to someone who thinks he is better or stronger than he really is and he needs to be 'taken down a peg.' *"He thinks that he is 'hot stuff' and he's become too big for his britches."*

Built like a brick shit house — alludes to an outdoor privy or toilet. Refers to someone who has a very sturdy physical build with straight lines. *"He must be a football lineman; he's built like a brick shit house."*

Best bib and tucker — alludes to bib overalls and a scarf like clothing worn on a woman's shoulders. Refers to semiformal dress. *"You wear your best bib and tucker when you go to their wedding dance."*

Dressed fancier than Lady Astor's horse — alludes to Lady Astor who was a well-known wealthy woman who adorned her horse extravagantly. Refers to someone who is overdressed for an occasion. *"She came to the dance dressed fancier than Lady Astor's horse."*

Fits like a saddle on a sow — alludes to a horse's saddle on a broad, short-legged female pig. Refers to someone whose clothing is ill fitting. *"That jacket fits you like a saddle on a sow."*

Mite nit tight — alludes to the tiny egg of a very small insect. Refers to something that is too small. *"Her jeans are a mite nit tight; don't you think?"*

Swallowed a watermelon seed — alludes to a large round melon. Refers to someone who is pregnant. *"Mrs. Jones has apparently swallowed a watermelon seed."*

When she walks, from the rear it looks like two tomcats fighting in a gunny sack — alludes to dynamic action or movement created by two male cats fighting in a confining, flexible burlap bag. Refers to a woman's rear that is dynamic and sexually attractive. *"When Judy walks by you, it looks like two tomcats fighting in a gunny sack."*

Stands out like a diamond in a goat's ass — alludes to a precious stone being passed by a goat that eats practically everything. Refers to someone or something with beauty or quality among the common or least attractive. *"Among the other girls, she stands out like a diamond in a goat's ass."*

Walking the dog — alludes to a lady accompanying a dog on a leash. Refers to a woman who makes an obvious effort to dress in a manner that displays her attributes for available men to observe. *"Since her husband died, she's been out walking the dog."*

She's no spring chicken — alludes to a young chicken or pullet compared to an old hen. Refers to a woman who is not full of energy and vitality. *"She may not be that old, but she's no spring chicken."*

Held together with bailing wire — alludes to flexible wire used to hold hay or straw bales together. Refers to ill-repaired machinery held together with bailing wire. (now-a-days it is duct tape) *"The old wagon is apt to fall apart; it appears to be held together with bailing wire."*

Flops around like a chicken with its head cut off — alludes to the act of chopping off the head of a chicken before butchering it and letting it jump about bleeding. Refers to someone who is clumsy and moves about loosely. *"When he dances, he flops about like a chicken with its head cut off."*

Thin as soup made from a starving sparrow — alludes to broth made from a very small bird that has not eaten. Refers to someone or something that is very slight or extraordinarily skinny. *"Since his illness, he looks as thin as soup made from a starving sparrow."*

So thin that you have to shake the sheets to find her — alludes to bed sheets with small flakes of skin. Refers to a woman who is extraordinarily skinny or emaciated. *"I wouldn't marry her; she's so thin you'd have to shake the sheets to find her."*

Grins like a cat that ate the canary — alludes to the satisfied look of a cat. Refers to someone who displays a broad smile of pleasure. *"After his success, he was grinning like the cat that ate the canary."*

Grins like a cat eatin' a cocklebur — alludes to a weed seed that is prickly and would irritate the lips of a cat. Refers to someone with a very broad smile. *"After she agreed to marry him, he grinned like a cat eatin' a cocklebur."*

Big as an ox — alludes to very large male cattle that are bred as a beast of burden. Refers to someone who has a very large and muscular frame. *"Don't mess with him; he is as big as an ox."*

Struts like the cock of the walk — alludes to a rooster proudly walking among 'his' flock of hens. Refers to someone who pompously walks about as if he/she is superior. *"After he got the job, he strutted around like the cock of the walk."*

Looks like death eatin' a soda cracker or death warmed over — alludes to a ghostly, thin figure. Refers to someone who is very pale and emaciated. *"Since he got out of the hospital, he has looked like death eatin' a cracker."*

Don't look up to snuff — alludes to pulverized tobacco that is inhaled through the nostrils. Refers to someone that has a bad cold or is ill. *"After the trip, she didn't look up to snuff."*

Fit as a fiddle — alludes to a well-tuned musical instrument. Refers to someone who appears healthy and active. *"He was ill, but now he is fit as a fiddle."*

Bleeding like a stuck hog — alludes to the butchering of a hog when they insert a knife into a main artery to drain the blood from the carcass. Refers to someone who is profusely bleeding. *"When the wire cut him, he bled like a stuck hog."*

Never be noticed on a galloping horse — alludes to a fast gait of a horse. Refers to a flaw or spot on clothing that really doesn't call attention to itself. *"Pay no mind to that little spot on your jacket; it will never be noticed on a galloping horse."*

Got a hitch in his getup — alludes to a horse that limps because its leg hit the hitch. Refers to someone that limps. *"She must have been hurt; she's got a hitch in her getup."*

Leaks like a sieve – alludes to a wire mesh utensil used for straining or sifting. Refers to something that leaks significantly. *"The boat was leaking like a sieve and was about to sink."*

Graceful as a hog on ice — alludes to the animal with short stocky legs that are difficult to control on slippery ice. Refers to someone who lacks harmony in movement. *"She came clopping in there with the grace of a pig on ice."*

Rough cut diamond — alludes to a precious stone that is poorly cut. Refers to someone who is attractive and delicate but behaves inappropriately and whose language is crude. *"Sally looks good but she's a rough cut diamond."*

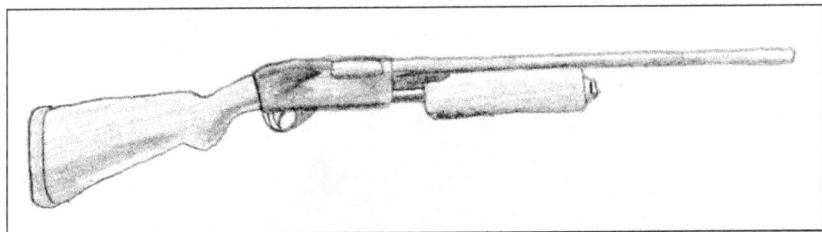

She's/he's so thin, she/he could bathe in a gun barrel — alludes to the barrel of a shotgun. Refers to someone who is tall and skinny. *"Jane is so thin; she could bathe in a gun barrel."*

Got a cow lick — alludes to a cow using its tongue in a circular movement to pull grass into its mouth. Refers to a spot on one's head where the hair grows in a circular pattern and is difficult to control by combing. *"He has nice hair except for his cow lick in the back of his head."*

Got a rooster tail — alludes to a male chicken's tail feathers that stand up in an unorthodox fashion. Refers to a spot on one's head where the hair sticks out in an unorthodox fashion and is difficult to control. *"They call him 'bed head' because of the two uncontrolled rooster tails on the back of his head."*

Bull in a china shop — alludes to a large and aggressive animal being put in a store that houses fragile and delicate dishes and glassware. Refers to someone who is extraordinarily large and awkward and out of place. *"At the formal banquet, he was like a bull in a china shop."*

Bright eyed and bushy tailed — alludes to a healthy squirrel or other animal. Refers to someone who is healthy and excited about life. *"Every morning Jan comes to work bright eyed and bushy tailed."*

Behaviors and *Dispositions*

Got a bur in his tail — alludes to a hunting dog that is frustrated by a cocklebur stuck in their tail. Refers to someone who appears agitated and angry. *"I don't know what is wrong with John, but he acts like he's got a bur in his tail."*

A hard dog to keep under the porch — alludes to a dog that constantly comes from its resting place to challenge whatever is there. Refers to someone who always interrupts the conversations or relationships with others. *"When the topic is politics, Ed is a hard dog to keep under the porch."*

Ought'a ring his neck — alludes to the method of killing chickens by grabbing its neck and circularly twisting its body. Refers to chastising someone severely. *"We ought'a ring his neck for pulling a stunt like that."*

Ruffles my feathers — alludes to a chicken when it gets upset or irritated. Refers to someone who is irritated by someone. *"I don't know why, but she really ruffles my feathers."*

Cut a rug — alludes to separating pieces of heavy fabric floor covering. Refers to someone dancing rapidly or violently. *"When they played the 1940's music, she really cuts a rug."*

Sticks in my craw — alludes to the gizzard, an organ in the digestive system of a chicken that contains sharp stone or gravel that grinds the ingested food into digestible pieces. Refers to a person who is perceived to be one who causes constant irritation, discontentment and discomfort. *"The way he acts sticks in my craw."*

Cock of the walk — alludes to the way the male chicken (rooster) struts around the hens in the flock. Refers to someone who puts on false airs. *"Because he has money, he struts around like the cock of the walk."*

Basket case — alludes to a wicker basket gurney that was used to transport or carry the dead, mentally deranged or physically impaired. Refers to someone who is mentally incapacitated or who is acting out of the ordinary way. *"He is a basket case over the divorce."*

Belly aching — alludes to a stomach ache. Refers to someone complaining or whining. *"The decision has been made; stop your belly aching."*

Happy as a cow in clover — alludes to a cow grazing on clover, one of its favorite foods but one that often causes the cow to bloat. Refers to a person's state of mind. *"When he saw her there, he was as happy as a cow in clover."*

Got an axe to grind — alludes to sharpening an axe on a grindstone. Refers to someone who has a grudge or is angry with someone. *"He did Jim wrong and now Jim has an axe to grind."*

Well oiled — alludes to machinery that is well lubricated. Refers to someone who has had too much alcohol to drink. *"Having spent the afternoon in the tavern, he was well oiled come evening."*

Rougher than a cob — alludes to the coarse texture of a dry field corncob, especially when it has to be used as a toiletry item. Refers to someone who is primitive or uncultured. *"Pete is rougher than a cob when it comes to polite conversation."*

Don't stew — alludes to meat and vegetables that are cooked slowly. Refers to extended worry or concern. *"It is going to happen; don't stew about it."*

Meaner than a settin' hen — alludes to a hen chicken sitting on her eggs to hatch them, and someone or something disturbs her. Refers to someone who gets very upset and mean. *"If I come home late she's meaner than a settin' hen."*

Madder than a wet hen — alludes to a hen chicken that does not like to get water on her. Refers to someone who is very angry and upset. *"He's madder than a wet hen at you."*

Meaner than a trapped badger — alludes to a nocturnal, carnivorous animal that is very aggressive. Refers to someone who is angry and aggressive. *"When you say anything bad about his kin, he gets meaner than a trapped badger."*

Meaner than a bitching sow at litter time — alludes to a female hog protecting her young pigs. Refers to someone who is very unhappy, aggressive and angry. *"In that situation, he is meaner than a bitching sow at litter time."*

Nervous as a cat in a room full of rocking chairs — alludes to an old-fashion rocking chair with naked rockers that could smash the cat's tail. Refers to someone or something that is very anxious or fears the worst. *"When he has to perform, he's as nervous as a cat in a room full of rocking chairs."*

Doing his chores — alludes to a farmer's daily responsibilities of feeding the chickens, slopping the hogs and milking the cow. Refers to someone who is following his daily routine of defecating. *"He'll be a while; he is doing his chores."*

Feelin' his barley-corn — alludes to ingredients in alcohol. Refers to someone who has overindulged in alcohol or is drunk. *"He came out of the tavern feelin' his barley-corn."*

Busy as a one-armed paperhanger with hives — alludes to someone who has one arm and is trying to hang wallpaper and scratch hives at the same time. Refers to someone who is very active in trying to do too many things at once. *"With her new responsibilities, she is as busy as a one-armed paperhanger with hives."*

Mad as a hornet — alludes to the disposition of a small stinging insect when its nest is disturbed. Refers to someone or something that is very angry. *"If Pete doesn't get his way, he is mad as a hornet."*

Got a cob up his butt — alludes to a rough, dry corncob. Refers to someone who is very irritated and upset. *"Most of the time, he acts like he's got a cob up his butt."*

To the hilt — alludes to the handle of a sword. Refers to the limit or completeness. *"She had it up to the hilt with his behavior."*

Came back with his tail between his legs — alludes to a dog that has been beaten or chastised. Refers to someone who has been severely criticized or beaten. *"The team came home with their tails between their legs after badly losing the game."*

Doesn't give a hoot — alludes to a common and frequent vocal expression of an owl. Refers to someone who does not care and is not interested. *"He doesn't give a hoot what happens."*

Stick in the mud — alludes to a tree branch that is stuck and almost buried in wet soil that makes it difficult to move. Refers to someone who is set in his/her ways –stubborn with a set attitude. *"She is being a stick in the mud and refuses to go with us."*

Three sheets in the wind — alludes to bed covers blowing every which way drying on a clothesline. Refers to someone who is intoxicated. *"Don't let him drive; he's three sheets in the wind."*

Going to hell in a hand basket — alludes to a wicker gurney or stretcher with two hand holes on either end for carrying. Refers to someone who is a significant sinner, who bypasses judgment day and who is destined for hell immediately after death. *"He has experienced sin at every turn of his life and is going to hell in a hand basket."*

Feeling his oats — alludes to a horse that becomes spirited after eating its favorite grain, oats. Refers to someone who is intoxicated. Also, feeling his barley/corn may be used. *"He's been drinking beer since noon and he's feeling his oats."*

Been bending his elbow — alludes to the act of drinking. Refers to someone who has had too much to drink. *"You can tell he's been down at the tavern bending his elbow."*

In her cups — alludes to drinking vessels. Refers to someone who is drunk. *"She's had too much booze; she's in her cups."*

Stubborn as a mule — alludes to an animal that is a crossbreed of a horse and a donkey and is well known for its obstinacy. Refers to someone who is unreasonable, and fixed in his/her opinion. *"You can't convince him of anything; he's as stubborn as a mule."*

Crestfallen — alludes to a rooster's fallen or drooping comb. Refers to someone who has been rejected, or one who is depressed or dispirited. *"Don came from the meeting crestfallen."*

About to tassel — alludes to the blossom at the top of the cornstalk that produces pollen for cross fertilization. Refers to children showing signs of puberty. *"She is twelve years old and about to tassel."*

Sweep your own porch first — alludes to sweeping a floor with a broom. Refers to someone who should check his/her own behavior before criticizing others. *"Sally needs to sweep her own porch before she criticizes others."*

Quiet as a mouse — alludes to a small rodent that sneaks about the house without making a sound. Refers to someone who is very reserved or has a quiet disposition. *"In a crowd she is as quiet as a mouse."*

Barking up the wrong tree — alludes to a hunting hound that mistakenly barks at the foot of the tree that does not shelter the raccoon. Refers to someone who makes errors in judgments and conclusions. *"In regards to this, you're barking up the wrong tree."*

Funny as a turd in the punch bowl — alludes to feces in a bowl containing a refreshing liquid. Refers to someone who is not a bit funny. *"His jokes are as funny as a turd in the punch bowl."*

Hot to trot — alludes to a gaited horse ready to move to a gait between a walk and a cantor. Refers to a woman who appears to want her relationships with males to progress more rapidly. *"She is hot to trot for him."*

Innocent as a lamb — alludes to baby sheep that are unpretentious and free from wrong doings. Refers to someone who appears not to have guilt or is free from wrong doings. *"Look at him standing by the broken door appearing as innocent as a lamb."*

A new broom sweeps clean — alludes to a broom made from natural bristles (broomcorn) that wear down with use. Refers to the behavior of a new hired man or employee and his dedicated effort on the job. *"Before you make a decision about Ed's work, remember that a new broom sweeps clean."*

Barking at the moon — alludes to a dog barking without cause or reason. Refers to someone who gets excited about anything and knows not about what he is speaking. *"Don't listen to Ted, he's known for barking at the moon."*

Shakes like a coon shittin' peach seeds — alludes to a raccoon that is trying to defecate a large seed. Refers to someone who is struggling and whose whole body shakes because of nerves. *"When he heard her coming, he shook like a coon shittin' a peach seed."*

Do what you want in the buggy, but don't startle the horses — alludes to a courting couple in a horse drawn four-wheeled carriage. Refers to warning a couple not to do anything that would cause the neighbors to gossip. *"I know you two are close, but don't do anything in the buggy that will startle the horses."*

Velvet bulldozer — alludes to a soft, smooth fabric and a caterpillar with a blade. Refers to someone who intimidates and/or gets his/her way in a delicate, soft manner. *"In this group, she performs like a velvet bulldozer."*

Chomping at the bit — alludes to a horse adjusting in its mouth the bit (controlling mouthpiece) to behind its teeth. Refers to someone who is eager and ready to go. *"He's chomping at the bit to get this project started."*

Exciting as watching paint dry — alludes to the inactive, static observation of an intangible process. Refers to a boring person who lacks dynamic involvement. *"Going to a party with him is as exciting as watching paint dry."*

Don't get your back up — alludes to a cat that when it gets upset or challenged it raises a hump in its back. Refers to someone who is about to be angry and aggressive. *"Don't get your back up over what he says."*

On the (water) wagon — alludes to the water wagon or cart used to dampen the dust on a town's main dirt streets. Refers to someone who has given up drinking alcohol, at least temporarily. *"He's on the wagon after he got his DWI."*

Like a dog chasing his own tail — alludes to a dog that runs around in circles trying to bite a flea or a bur from its tail. Refers to someone who appears to be going in circles while trying to solve a problem or situation. *"The solution to his problem eludes him, and he appears to be like a dog that chases its own tail."*

Jumpy as a grasshopper in a chicken house — alludes to an insect that jumps especially in the confines of a small building while being pursued by chickens that enjoy eating grasshoppers. Refers to someone who is very nervous about a situation. *"In his interview, he was as jumpy as a grasshopper in a chicken house."*

A straw in the wind — alludes to a stem of wheat that is very light and easy to blow away. Refers to someone who is unpredictable in his/her behavior. *"If she would settle down, she'd be ok, but she's a straw in the wind."*

Don't mix your meat with your potatoes — alludes to table manners or etiquette. Refers to advice to someone not to mix their social or personal lives with their work and their workplace. *"They have been flirting with each other during work breaks; they should know better than to mix their meat with their potatoes."*

Takes a good horse to fart at the end of the day — alludes to a workhorse that has been worked so hard it shouldn't even have the energy to pass gas. Refers to someone who is still energetic after a day's manual labor. *"I'm surprised that he still wants to go to the dance after working all day; you know it takes a good horse to fart at the end of the day."*

Jumped the traces — alludes to a harnessed horse that steps out of the leather straps that connect it with a cart or wagon. Refers to someone who becomes independent and disregards responsibilities. *"She jumped the traces with this project."*

Cool as a cucumber — alludes to a cylindrical fruit that is dark green in color. Refers to someone who maintains his/her composure under duress. *"During the birth of their child, she remained cool as a cucumber."*

Don't hang your rags on my bush — alludes to dirty clothes put out to air on a bush. Refers to someone who frequently wants to share his/ her woes and concerns. *"Don't hang your rags on my bush; I've got enough problems of my own."*

Don't beat around the bush — alludes to a hunter who beats around the bush when the game birds are in the bush. Refers to someone who hesitates in making a decision or being assertive. *"Don't beat around the bush, come out and tell him what you think."*

Keep your nose out of it — alludes to a dog that sniffs around in most circumstances. Refers to someone who curiously interrupts others with questions. *"That is none of your business; so, you should keep your nose out of it."*

Curiosity killed the cat — alludes to a feline that finds many things that excite their interest. Refers to someone who shows intense interest in events and others. *"Joe should not be asking all those questions about her; curiosity killed the cat."*

Catting around —alludes to a tomcat on the prowl for a female companion. Refers to someone who goes out to bars and flirts with the opposite sex. *"John spends most of his evenings out cating around."*

Cut from the same cloth – alludes to sewing two garments from the same piece of material. Refers to two people who have the same characteristics or behaviors. *"Those two women are cut from the same cloth."*

Happy as a pig in mud on a hot summer day — alludes to a pig that does not sweat and uses mud as a cooling agent. Refers to someone who is very comfortable and content. *"Look at Harry smile; he's as happy as a pig in mud on a hot summer day."*

You just as well partake of the devil as to taste of his broth — alludes to the Biblical inference that to think about a sin is as bad as committing it. Refers to someone who lusts for another's spouse. *"Look at Tom flirting with Ed's wife, he just as well partake of the devil as to taste of his broth."*

Happy as a lark — alludes to a small singing bird (meadowlark). Refers to someone who is content and expresses it. *"She is vibrant and appears to be happy as a lark."*

You attract more flies with honey than you do with vinegar — alludes to an insect and its attraction to something sweet rather than something sour. Refers to the concept that people are attracted to a sweet and wholesome person rather than one with a sour disposition. *"You should be kind and caring rather than indifferent; you attract more flies with honey than you do with vinegar."*

Wilder than a March hare — alludes to a rabbit during mating season. Refers to someone who is socially active and parties a lot. *"At the dance, he was wilder than a March hare."*

Hog wild — alludes to a hog that when cornered or threatened will react in an intense, unpredictable manner. Refers to someone who becomes very excited and impulsive. *"When she heard about his promotion, she went hog wild."*

Bitter as gall — alludes to an alkaline fluid that is found in the gallbladder that aids in digestion of food. Refers to someone who is resentful and cynical in behavior. *"When she did not get the appointment, she became bitter as gall."*

Get in the buggy or wagon — alludes to a command to board a horse-drawn carriage. Refers to a strong request to conform or join the others in a belief or action. *"Everyone is going; get in the buggy."*

Can't make a silk purse out of a sow's ear — alludes to a pig's ear that is rough and tough. Refers to trying to refine an uncultured and crude person. *"Give up! Dick will never be a refined person. You can't make a silk purse out of a sow's ear."*

Don't try to get in without a ticket — alludes to a card or paper indicating permission to be admitted. Refers to a warning to someone not to get involved in matters that do not pertain to him/her without a proper invitation. *"That is a personal matter: don't try to get in without a ticket."*

We come with our hats in our hands — alludes to removal of one's head cover before entering the doorway. Refers to an apology for a wrongdoing. *"We come with our hats in our hands in regards to your name's omission on the guest list."*

Who pulled your chain? — alludes to a chain on a light fixture. Refers to an insulting question in regards to an unsolicited remark. *"Who pulled your chain in regards to the party?"*

The loudest tomcat on the fence gets the action — alludes to a male cat during mating season. Refers to advice to someone who remains quiet when there is a favor to be gained. *"Speak up in the meeting; it's the loudest tomcat on the fence that gets the action."* Also, the squeaky wheel gets the grease is used as a similar reference.

Marriage and *Separation*

Got a lemon in the garden of love —
alludes to the sour fruit that is a poor choice among the other sweeter fruits. Refers to a poor choice in regards to marriage partners. *"When she married him, she got a lemon in the garden of love for he is worthless as teats on a boar."*

Went for a roll in the hay — alludes to physically lying and rolling on and in a stack of cut grass. Refers to a couple who have had sexual relations. *"He's marrying her after they went for a roll in the hay."*

Tied the knot — alludes to uniting two pieces of string or rope. Refers to a couple's wedding. *"Emily and Dan tied the knot last Friday."*

Give her a washboard and a mirror so she can watch herself starve to death — alludes to a frame with a corrugated surface upon which clothes are rubbed. The washboard was used by poor people who couldn't afford washing machines. Refers to someone who married someone who was believed not to be able to properly support her financially. *"When she married him, you just as well have given her a mirror with her washboard; so she can watch herself starve to death."*

Drove her ducks to a poor market — alludes to the selling of ducks for less than they were worth. Refers to someone who could have married someone who was more attractive and wealthy. *"She drove her ducks to a poor market when she married him."*

Why buy the cow when you can get the milk free? — alludes to getting the cow's milk without responsibility for the cow. Refers to a man who has the sexual and social privileges of a woman without marrying her. *"He's not going to marry her; why buy the cow when you can get the milk free?"*

She led him down the primrose path — alludes to an early blossoming yellow flower that often borders a walkway. Refers to someone whose future promises in marriage are superficial. *"Before he married her, she had led him down the primrose path where everything is beautiful."*

Stripped him/her clean — alludes to milking a cow and the person doing the milking squeezes all the milk possible from each teat. Refers to someone who takes everything possible from another. *"During the divorce proceeding, she stripped him clean of all their assets."*

Gave him the boot — alludes footwear to a kick. Refers to someone who forcefully removes a man from a marriage. *"She took him to court and gave him the boot."*

Mended their fences — alludes to repairing the wire to make the fence stock tight. Refers to a couple that has settled their differences. *"Bob and Mary have mended their fences and are back together."*

You have to please the cow to get to the heifer calf — alludes to the mother of the calf and her willingness to relinquish her calf. Refers to someone pleasing the mother in order to marry her daughter. *"She'll be your mother-in-law and you'll have to please the cow to get to the heifer calf."*

What is good for the goose is good for the gander — alludes to the female and male goose. Refers to someone justifying a man's behavior based on what a woman has done. *"He should go with her; what is good for the goose is good for the gander."*

Split the blanket — alludes to severing a bed covering into two pieces. Refers to a kind way of saying the highly connotative word 'divorce.' *"After three years of marriage, they split the blanket."*

Left holding the bag — alludes to someone who is left holding an empty sack. Refers to someone who has taken the material content of a marriage and left the partner with nothing of consequence. *"She took off with all their financial savings and left him holding the bag."*

On the rocks — alludes to a vessel coming aground and ending the voyage. Refers to the ending of a marriage. *"I hear that their marriage is on the rocks."*

Flew the coup — alludes to an old hen chicken escaping from the culling coup or cage. Refers to someone who escapes marriage by leaving. *"After their fight, she flew the coup."*

Hen pecked — alludes to a hen chicken pecking at other chickens with her beak. Refers to a wife who nags her husband and dictates what he can do. *"He is so hen pecked, she won't let him go with us."*

Clipped his wings — alludes to cutting the wing feathers of domestic fowl to prevent them from flying over the fence. Refers to a wife's actions in restricting the husband's behavior. *"They were married only two months and she clipped his wings."*

She put a ring in his nose — alludes to the ring the farmer clips in a hog's snout to prevent the hog from rooting the soil and escaping under a fence. Refers to a wife who restricts her husband's behavior. *"Harry used to be a 'rounder' but his wife put a ring in his nose."*

Don't crap too near the cabin — alludes to defecating near one's living quarters and contaminating the area. Refers to advice to a person not to misbehave or commit adultery too near his/her community. *"She divorced him, after he crapped too near the cabin and got caught."*

He crapped in his own nest — alludes to a bird that defecates in its own nest and causes an unpleasant situation. Refers to someone who has caused an unpleasant situation in his/her home. *"He crapped in his own nest when he had the hired girl move in with them."*

Got hitched — alludes to fastening of a horse to a wagon or post. Refers to a couple that was united in marriage. *"Bob and Mary got hitched some time ago."*

Better dance with the one who brought her — alludes to dancing with the person with whom she came. Refers to a wife who should attend to her husband and not other men. *"Look at her flirt; she better dance with the one who brought her."*

She shortened his stake rope —
alludes to tying a horse or
cow with a rope and a stake to
restrict its grazing area. Refers
to a wife making restrictions
on her husband's activities.
*"After their marriage, she shortened
his stake rope."*

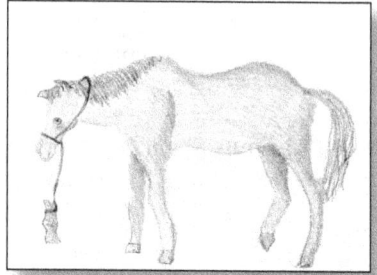

Cuts a wide swath — alludes to a
farmer who cuts grass hay with a scythe and swings it widely. Refers to
someone who is sexually active over a wide territory. *"Even though he is
married he cuts a wide swath."*

In the doghouse — alludes to a small building housing a yard dog. Refers to
a husband who is in trouble with his wife. *"He got himself in the doghouse
over last night's poker game."*

Landed on a turd — alludes to falling on fecal matter. Refers to someone
marrying a very poor choice. *"When she married him she landed on a turd."*

Colder than a mother–in–law's kiss — alludes to a wife's mother's
relationship with her son-in-law. Refers to a distant and poor
relationship or response. *"She treats him colder than a mother-in-law's kiss."*

Took the plunge — alludes to diving into a substance wholeheartedly. Refers
to the commitment of marriage. *"She knew what he was like before she took
the plunge."*

The dance ain't over until the fiddler quits fiddling — alludes to a
partnership commitment. Refers to a marriage separation. *"You can't
divorce him now; the dance ain't over until the fiddler quits fiddling."*

Common Sense

Still water runs deep — alludes to pools of water within a stream that appear deep and has less obvious current. Refers to a quiet person whose thoughts are more complex and complete even though he/she isn't always talking. *"She is intelligent even though she has little to say; still water runs deep, you know."*

An empty wagon rattles — alludes to a wooden wagon drawn by a horse over rough roads. Refers to someone who is constantly talking but knows not about what he/she speaks. *"He doesn't know what he is talking about; you know an empty wagon rattles."*

Talking through his hat —alludes to someone holding his hat in front of his mouth. Refers to someone talking nonsense or bragging. *"On most topics you'll find he's talking through his hat."*

Ain't had no fetching up — alludes to the menial task of a dog retrieving something. Refers to someone who is uneducated especially in manners. *"He eats like he ain't had no fetching up."*

Hayseed — alludes to the seed and chaff of grasses that cling to clothing while one is putting up hay. Refers to someone who is 'backward' or a 'bumpkin.' *"He's been on the farm his whole life and ain't had no fetching up; in other words he's a real hayseed."*

Don't know sic um from cum err — alludes to a command to a dog to go after something or a command to come back. Refers to someone who does not understand a menial task. *"You have to feel sorry for him; he don't know sic um from cum err."*

Don't know if she's washin' or hangin' out — alludes to someone who is either washing clothes or hanging them out on a line to dry. Refers to someone who is unaware and does not understand the current circumstances. *"Socially, the poor girl doesn't know if she's washin' or hangin' out."*

Not dry behind the ears — alludes to a new born animal that still has mucus behind its ears. Refers to an immature youth. *"He can't handle the responsibility; he's not dry behind the ears."*

He don't know enough not to piss against the wind — alludes to the act of urinating outdoors against the wind and having the urine blow back on him. Refers to someone who lacks basic common sense. *"Don't count on him for help; he don't know enough not to piss against the wind."*

Don't know shit from Shinola — alludes to the difference in feces and a brand of shoe polish. Refers to someone who cannot discriminate among the simplest things. *"Don't ask him; he don't know shit from Shinola."*

Don't know Jack shit —alludes to someone who doesn't know the least bit of information. Refers to someone who is naïve and unaware of the circumstances. *"You don't know Jack shit about what's going on right before your eyes."*

Don't know heads from tails — alludes to the head and the tail of an animal or a coin. Refers to someone who is naïve. *"Don't let him make the decision; he don't know heads from tails."*

Couldn't find his butt with both hands — alludes to the task of feeling one's own rectum. Refers to someone who not only is lacking mentally but also lacks dexterity. *"Don't choose him for our team; he couldn't find his butt with both hands."*

A few bricks short of a full load — alludes to a cart carrying clay bricks that is not completely filled. Refers to someone who lacks intelligence. *"She couldn't figure out the problem; you know she's a few bricks short of a full load."*

Three pickles short of a full quart — alludes to a jar containing cucumbers preserved in a quart jar. Refers to someone who lacks intelligence and common sense. *"She has trouble with understanding the situation; she's three pickles short of a full quart."*

Barking at a knot in a rope — alludes to a dog barking at a plaything. Refers to someone who fusses or makes an issue of unimportant things. *"He shouldn't be worried; he's barking at a knot in a rope."*

Only one oar in the water — alludes to one of two wooden implements used to propel and steer a boat. Refers to someone who lacks intelligence and/or the ability to control his own thoughts or expression. *"You can't expect him to know; he's only got one oar in the water."*

Bubble off plumb — alludes to an instrument, a level, that is used to determine true exact perpendicular and vertical alignment. Refers to someone who thinks and acts in an unorthodox manner. *"You can't tell what he'll do; he's a bubble off plumb."*

Crazy as a loon — alludes to a waterfowl that is unpredictable in both behavior and expression. Refers to someone who is perceived as being mentally ill. *"Don't listen to him; he's crazy as a loon."*

Got toys in the attic — alludes to childhood toys that are stored in an area of the house beneath the roof. Refers to someone who is childish, simple and unpredictable. *"She's not dependable; she's got toys in her attic."*

Shuckin or scoopin' — alludes to the process of removing ears of field corn the stalks and loading the ears from the wagon with a scoop shovel. Refers to someone who lacks awareness or is naïve. *"The poor man doesn't know if he is shuckin or scoopin."*

Got bats in the belfry — alludes to nocturnal flying mammals inhabiting a bell tower. Refers to someone who is mentally disturbed. *"He's not responsible for his behavior; he's got bats in his belfry."*

Went haywire — alludes to flexible and spring-like wire used to bind hay bales. Refers to a person or situation that is uncontrollable or is confusing. *"When he heard the news, he went haywire."*

Practical as a wheel-barrow with rope handles — alludes to a cart that is pushed by lifting handles in order to transport loads. Refers to someone or something that is not useful or logical. *"When it comes to spending money, he is as practical as a wheelbarrow with rope handles."*

If his brains were dynamite, he wouldn't have enough to blow his nose — alludes to a volatile explosive inside one's head. Refers to someone who lacks mental ability. *"He's not very smart; in fact if his brains were dynamite, he wouldn't have enough to blow his nose."*

All wet — alludes to someone who has been dowsed with water. Refers to someone who has little knowledge and is naïve. *"When it comes to sailing a boat, he is all wet."*

Pages are stuck together — alludes to a book that has a page or two adhered to a preceding page. Refers to someone who does not make sense at times or is not consistent in his thinking. *"It is difficult to understand him; he's got some pages stuck together."*

Got a screw loose — alludes to a fastener that is not tight. Refers to someone who suffers a mental illness. *"The way she acts; you'd think she has a screw loose."*

She's off her rocker — alludes to a rocking chair that has lost one of its rockers. Refers to someone who supposedly is mentally ill. *"She's not responsible for her actions; she's off her rocker."*

Credibility

He wears the hat, but he ain't got the cattle — alludes to someone who wears a cowboy hat, but has no cattle. Refers to someone who acts as if he is financially well off, but he is not. *"He don't have a pot to pee in; he wears the hat, but he don't have the cattle."*

He'll go to the poor farm in a Cadillac — alludes to someone who is financially destitute and has been admitted to the "county poor farm," but for show he/she is delivered first class. Refers to someone who pretends he is something he is not. *"He is a deceptive showman who will likely go to the poor farm in a Cadillac."*

He plows a straight furrow — alludes to a farmer who prepares to plant a field crop in long straight rows. Refers to someone who is predictably honest and credible. *"You can trust him; he plows a straight furrow."*

Phony as a three-dollar bill — alludes to currency that doesn't exist. Refers to someone who pretends to be something he isn't. *"Don't believe what he says; he's as phony as a three-dollar bill."*

Cut the ice — alludes to the cutting of ice on a pond to be used for refrigeration. Refers to someone who could not fulfill his duties or responsibilities. *"He tried hard, but he just couldn't cut the ice with his new job."*

There's a lot of frosting on that cake — alludes to the fluffy, sugar-coated substance that covers a cake. Refers to someone whose true self is disguised with a superficial appearance. *"You have to get to know Joe; there's a lot of frosting on that cake."*

Cunning as a fox — alludes to a small, wild canine animal that preys on chickens and their eggs. Refers to someone who is sly and crafty in his/her dealings with others and should not be trusted. *"Beware of him in your financial dealings; he is cunning as a fox."*

Egg on his/her face — alludes to a fox or dog that comes out of a chicken house after eating the forbidden eggs. Refers to someone who has been caught doing wrong. *"He came out of that deal with egg on his face."*

Letting the fox guard the chicken house — alludes to the fox that eats both chickens and their eggs. Refers to someone who has selfish motives and takes particular responsibilities. *"Putting her in charge of the money is like letting the fox guard the chicken house."*

Sweeps a lot under the rug — alludes to a broom sweeping dirt under the rug to give the area a clean appearance. Refers to someone who hides or conceals information. *"In regards to that case, the authorities apparently swept some of the evidence under the rug."*

Gave him the key to the front door — alludes to having someone with access to an entrance to private property that could be observed. Refers to the granting of trust to someone. *"He let them down after they trusted him. They figuratively gave him the key to the front door."*

Gave him free rein — alludes to the straps attached to the bit with which a horse is controlled. Refers to giving someone freedom to do what he/she chooses. *"She was given free rein of the bank's investments."*

Slippery as a greased pig — alludes to a contest in which a pig is greased and contestants try to catch and hold it. Contests were held at community picnics or fairs. Refers to someone's poor accountability and responsibility. *"Double check your contract; Harry is slippery as a greased pig."*

Handy as a pocket on your bib-overalls — alludes to the number of pockets in a farmer's outer garment – bib-overalls. Refers to someone who is capable of fixing or repairing many things. *"Call John; he's as handy as a pocket on your bib-overalls."*

He'd steal the pennies off a dead man's eyes — alludes to the practice of putting pennies on the eyes of a dead man to keep them closed. Refers to someone who goes to no end to get money. *"You can't trust him; he'd steal the pennies off a dead man's eyes."*

Straight arrow — alludes to a straight, thin shaft with a point at one end and stabilizing vanes on the other. Refers to an honest and law abiding person. *"She couldn't have stolen it; she is a straight arrow."*

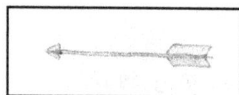

He's so crooked, they'll have to screw him into the ground when they bury him — alludes to an auger used to bore postholes. Refers to someone who is dishonest and not trustworthy. *"You can't trust him; he's so crooked, they'll have to screw him into the ground when they bury him."*

Crooked as a dog's hind leg — alludes to the shape of a dog's hind leg. Refers to someone who would cheat you and is not trustworthy. *"Watch out for him; he's crooked as a dog's hind leg."*

Even his dog won't come to dinner when he calls — alludes to a favorable command by a dog's master. Refers to someone who is not believable or trustworthy. *"You can't believe a thing he says; even his dog won't come to dinner when he calls."*

In a pig's eye — alludes to the narrow focus of vision with little peripheral sight and the inflexible head of swine. Refers to an event or behavior that is unlikely to be observed. *"I'll vote for him in a pig's eye."*

Situations and Tasks

Don't get the cart before the horse — alludes to a horse-drawn cart. Refers to the inappropriate organization of a task. *"First things first; don't get the cart before the horse."*

Cut and dried — alludes to hay/grass that has been mowed, dried and ready to process. Refers to a task that is complete and ready to put into effect. *"That decision was cut and dried before we even heard about it."*

It'll all come out in the wash — alludes to stains in the material being washed. Refers to facts and evidence that will be brought out in the discussion. *"You have only heard part of the information; it'll all come out in the wash."*

In the bag — alludes to a hunter who stores his dead birds in a game bag. Refers to someone who has successfully accomplished a task or deal. *"He's got the contract in the bag."*

Hit the nail on the head — alludes to a hammer striking a nail directly on the head. Refers to the correct assumption. *"Harry hit the nail on the head with that comment."*

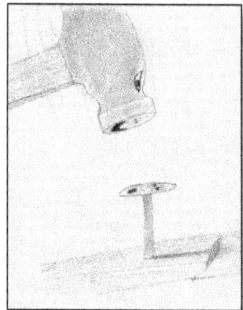

Keep your nose to the grindstone — alludes to a stone wheel used to sharpen tools or implements. Refers to diligent and concerted effort toward completing a task. *"Don't give up; keep your nose to the grindstone and you'll succeed."*

Got her tit in the wringer — alludes to a woman who leans over an old-fashioned clothes washing wringer that is hand cranked and she gets her breast in between the rollers. Refers to someone who gets caught doing something wrong. *"She got her tit in the wringer over that episode."*

To harness — alludes to applying the leather straps that control a horse pulling a cart or wagon. Refers to capturing and controlling something. *"They hope to harness the wind for energy."*

Snake in the grass — alludes to an unforeseen and discomforting appearance of a snake encountered while walking in the pasture or while putting up hay. Refers to an unexpected hidden element that is usually adverse. *"Watch what you say and do; there may be a snake in the grass."*

Like boar pork — alludes to pork from a male swine that had not been castrated within eight weeks after birth; the testosterone permeates the meat and gives it a bad smell and taste when cooked. Refers to a distasteful situation. *"That whole situation is like boar pork to me."*

Use a stick or a carrot — alludes to methods of punishment or treat rewards used to motivate a horse. Refers to means to control or motivate someone. *"To get them to see our point of view, we need to use a stick or a carrot."*

Face the music — alludes to experiencing a musical band both visually as well as audibly. Refers to someone who needs to admit his/her wrong doing and accept the punishment. *"You broke the law and now you need to face the music."*

The last straw — alludes to the light and insignificant chaff of wheat. Refers to a small thing added to many other significant things that are the causes for change. *"His resentful back talk was the last straw and he was fired."*

Ten miles of mud road — alludes to roads that are not hard surfaced and when it rains the wheels of the wagon or vehicle get stuck. Refers to a very difficult task to accomplish. *"Getting an agreement is like traveling on ten miles of mud road up hill."*

Water over the dam — alludes to confined water spilling over the dam that is containing it. Refers to actions or decisions that have already been taken or made. *"The decisions made at our last meeting are water over the dam."*

Too many irons in the fire — alludes to a blacksmith who has too many pieces of iron in the forge to handle. Refers to someone who is trying to do too many things at one time. (multitasking) *"She is an excellent manager, but she has too many irons in the fire."*

More than one way to skin a skunk — alludes to the difficulty of taking the fur from a skunk without disturbing the odor causing glands. Refers to taking a different approach to a situation. *"Your way is alright, but there is more than one way to skin a skunk."*

Slim pickins — alludes to a poor crop harvest or production below average yield. Refers to the lack of choices. *"She had slim pickins when it came to choosing a husband."*

Threw a wrench into the engine — alludes to a tool thrown into an operating engine causing it to stop or malfunction. Refers to someone or something that disrupts or alters a task. *"Even just her presence throws a wrench into the engine."*

The pigs are out — alludes to pigs escaping from their confinement and with their independent nature they run in different directions. Refers to an uncontrollable situation with the participants each having a different agenda. *"In the last board meeting the pigs got out."*

Missed a good lick — alludes to a cow licking a salt block. Refers to missing an excellent opportunity. *"He missed a good lick when he walked away from the conversation."*

Like pushing a log chain uphill — alludes to a heavy but very flexible steel chain. Refers to a practically impossible task. *"Getting her to change her attitude is like pushing a log chain uphill."*

Works like a dog — alludes to a hunting dog that works hard at discovering and flushing game birds from the brush. Refers to someone who is diligent and works hard at the task. *"He worked like a dog on that project."*

Take the bull by the horns — alludes to a male ox and the best way to subdue it. Refers to facing a situation head on and directly. *"Under these circumstances, you'll have to take the bull by the horns in order to get anything done."*

Too late to shut the gate after the horses are out — alludes to confined horses that have escaped through an opened gate. Refers to a situation that has already occurred and nothing can be altered by trying to retract the events. *"The deal is closed and it's too late to shut the gate after the horses are already out."*

Don't step over the horse to get to the fly — alludes to disturbing a large horse to get to an insignificant insect. Refers to ignoring the large problems and focusing on small ones. *"We have important matters to attend to rather than these small ones; don't step over the horse to get to the fly."*

Tighter than a bull's ass during fly season — alludes to male cattle closing the anal sphincter muscle to limit the attraction of flies. Refers to a bolt or machine part that is rusted or corroded and extremely difficult to remove. *"The bolt that secures the hinge is tighter than a bull's ass during fly season."*

Difficult as pickin' fly shit out of pepper — alludes to the insect that has feces the same color, size and shape as ground pepper. Refers to an impossible task. *"Finding solutions to the problems is as difficult as pickin' fly shit out of pepper."*

Don't beat a dead horse — alludes to attempting to get action from a horse that is dead. Refers to trying to resolve a situation that has already been handled in a different way. *"Trying to rehash our decision is like beating a dead horse."*

Water off a duck's back — alludes to the feathers on a duck that are water repellent. Refers to an issue that is ignored completely. *"They treated that issue like water off a duck's back."*

Down to brass tacks — alludes to furniture upholstery fasteners. Refers to specific and basic points of the issue. *"Let's get to the brass tacks in regard to the problem."*

Opened a can of worms — alludes to a tin can filled with earthworms that when opened the worms all try to escape. Refers to broaching a subject that soon becomes uncontrollable. *"When he mentioned the subject of responsibilities, he opened a can of worms."*

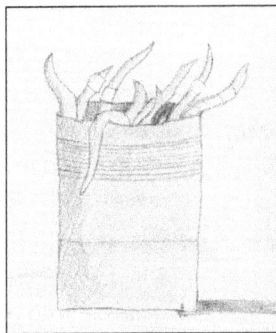

You can lead a horse to water but you can't make it drink — alludes to providing something for an animal but the animal must do the partaking. Refers to a situation in which something is provided but the participants must do the partaking. *"We've done all we can to get them involved; you can lead a horse to water but you can't make it drink."*

Don't cut off the limb you're sittin' on — alludes to trimming a tree. Refers to ignoring or not attending to past events. *"Be careful about how you handle the situation; don't cut off the limb you're sittin' on."*

Don't burn your bridges — alludes to bridges that serve as escape routes. Refers to maintaining past associations and relationships. *"Avoid angering them; you don't want to burn your bridges before the project is complete."*

The grass is always greener on the other side of the fence — alludes to a grazing animal that tries to get through the fence to get the grass on the other side. Refers to someone who thinks that other people and other situations are always better. *"She is envious of her and her position; you know for her the grass is always greener on the other side of the fence."*

Bitter pill to swallow — alludes to medicine that has a sharp unpleasant taste. Refers to an unpleasant decision or statement. *"The new farm guidelines are bitter pills to swallow."*

Get your ducks lined up in a row — alludes to ducks that follow their leader in a straight line. Refers to necessary organization. *"Get your ducks lined up in a row before you proceed."*

Snowball's chance in hell — alludes to the hot fire of hell melting a snowball. Refers to something that has very little chance of succeeding. *"She has a snowball's chance in hell of getting the crops out before the first snow."*

Too thick to stir — alludes to liquid in a bowl. Refers to a situation that is very complicated. *"That relationship is too thick to stir."*

Went whole hog — alludes to butchering and using all of the hog's body parts. Refers to attending to all aspects and completing them. *"They went whole hog on that project."*

From the frying pan into the fire — alludes to a frying pan with hot grease spilled into an open fire. Refers to someone who is in trouble and gets further in trouble. *"She jumped from the frying pan into the fire with that comment."*

Don't bite off more than you can chew — alludes to taking into your mouth more than you can process. Refers to someone trying to do too much at one time. *"Focus your energy and don't bite off more than you can chew."*

A fly in the soup or ointment — alludes to an insect in either edible soup or medical ointment. Refers to a problem that needs to be dealt with before continuing the process. *"Her statement put a fly in the ointment."*

Behind the eight ball — alludes to a pool game in which the last ball to be made is the eight ball. Refers to a very precarious situation. *"They got him behind the eight ball on that deal."*

Tar and feather — alludes to a dark, oily and sticky substance created by the destructive distillation of coal and the body covering of foul that was applied to the skin of an individual as a means of punishment. Refers to very strong criticism. *"Because he boasted of his superiority, they tarred and feathered him at the meeting."*

Like finding a needle in a haystack — alludes to a sewing needle that has the same size and shape as stems of hay piled high in a field. Refers to a very difficult task. *"Trying to find common ground is like finding a needle in a haystack."*

Like plowing new ground — alludes to using a plow, an implement, used to make furrows in grassland that may contain unexpected large rocks. Refers to a difficult and time-consuming task. *"We don't know what will happen; we're plowing new ground."*

One bird in the hand is worth two in the bush — alludes to game bird hunting. Refers to a situation where one has something rather than anticipating what he/she might get. *"Settle for what you got; a bird in the hand is worth two in the bush."*

Made from scratch — alludes to beginning something without combined materials. Refers to developing or mixing materials without having material pre-mixed or made. *"She made the cake from scratch."*

Let Eloise make the gravy — alludes to the person who makes the best sauce from meat broth. Refers to the practice of letting the person with the most experience and/or expertise do each part of a task. *"Joe should build the frame; you know the old saying: let Eloise make the gravy."*

Slick as snot on a doorknob — alludes to the slick nature of nose mucus. Refers to an easy task that is completed well. *"You did that slick as snot on a doorknob."*

Don't cry over spilled milk — alludes to a child spilling milk at the table. Refers to someone who is very upset about a mistake that was made. *"It's too late to worry about it; don't cry over spilled milk."*

Trying to nail Jello to a tree — alludes to a brand of gelatin which has no substance and quivers. Refers to a very difficult, if not impossible, task. *"Building the shed without nails is about like trying to nail Jello to a tree."*

Easy as duck soup — alludes to when a duck is cooked, it releases fatty juices that make soup. Refers to something that is natural and takes little effort. *"Fastening the two sheets is easy as duck soup."*

Fish or cut bait — alludes to the practice of diverting one's attention from fishing. Refers to someone who has been challenged for not sticking to the task at hand. *"With this project, you ought to either fish or cut bait."*

Let sleeping dogs lie — alludes to an outdoor watchdog that is asleep. Refers to ignoring a related problem that may resolve itself in the process without attention. *"We don't need to discuss that situation; let sleeping dogs lie."*

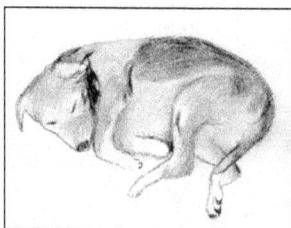

There is water in the well, but you're using the wrong bucket — alludes to an open water well that one dips into in order to retrieve some water. Refers to an easy task complicated by an inappropriate procedure. *"He is going at the problem the wrong way; there is water in the well, but he is using the wrong bucket."*

Slipped through the cracks — alludes to some small object falling through a crack in the floor. Refers to some subject that was not appropriately discussed. *"The topic of reciprocation slipped through the cracks."*

The other side of the coin — alludes to two sides of a coin: heads and tails. Refers to an argument in which there are two sides to consider. *"On the other side of the coin, we may not be financially capable of doing it."*

Scratched the surface — alludes to a slight abrasion of one material by another. Refers to a superficial coverage of a problem or subject. *"At the last meeting, we hardly scratched the surface of the subject."*

If the dog hadn't stopped to crap, he'd caught the rabbit — alludes to a dog that stopped to defecate while the rabbit kept on running. Refers to something hypothetical which could have happened. *"Sure you could have done it; just like the dog if it hadn't stopped, it could have caught the rabbit."*

Time, Distance and Weather

Bat out of hell — alludes to a flying nocturnal mammal flying out of the eternal fires of hell. Refers to a quick movement or exit.
"She drove like a bat out of hell to get away from the dangerous situation."

The apple will fall when it's time — alludes to ripe fruit and when it detaches itself from the tree. Refers to the act of rushing into doing something before preparations have been made. *"Wait to do that; the apple will fall from the tree when it's time."*

Two shakes of a dog's tail — alludes to a dog moving its tail rapidly. Refers to a very short period of time. *"I'll be with you in two shakes of a dog's tail."*

Hold your horses — alludes to holding the horse reins tightly. Refers to advising someone to be patient, "don't get into a toot" and don't start the task immediately. *"Hold your horses; we have time to get the job done."*

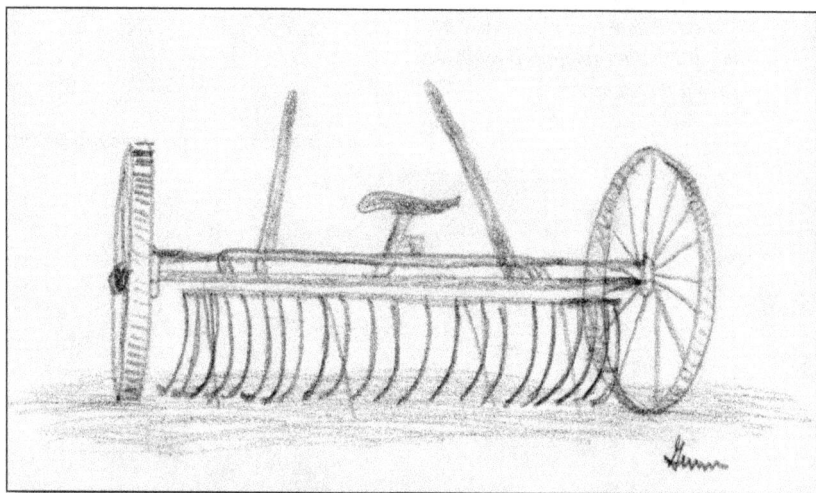

Make hay while the sun shines — alludes to the appropriate time to cut and stack or bale grasses. Refers to the appropriate time to do something. *"Let's go and do it today; you know one should make hay while the sun shines."*

Nip it in the bud — Alludes to pinching off a leaf or flower before the plant spreads. Refers to stopping a situation before it gets out of control. *"Before that behavior gets established, we need to nip it in the bud."*

My coffee is saucered and blewed — alludes to the way one cools his/her cup of coffee. Refers to the concept that a person is ready to go or do something. *"My coffee is saucered and blewed and I am ready to get on with it."*

Don't take long to curry a pony — alludes to the length of time it takes to comb a small horse. Refers to the amount of time it will take to complete a small task. *"We can do the project now; it don't take long to curry a pony."*

Quick as a wink — alludes to the movement of an eye-lid. Refers to a very short time period. *"We can have that finished quick as a wink."*

Goin' to town — alludes to the excitement of farmwives and children when they are getting ready to make a trip to town to sell their produce and shop. Refers to someone who acts quickly or in an excited manner. *"He is really going to town with his sale of cars."*

Moving at a snail's pace — alludes to a small, slow moving mollusk. Refers to something that is developing or moving at a very slow rate. *"That whole project is moving at a snail's pace."*

A stitch in time saves nine — alludes to one good, deliberate stitch in clothing repair will save nine stitches later. Refers to the concept that one should do the job slowly and accurately the first time. *"Don't rush your job; a stitch in time saves nine."*

Strike while the iron is hot — alludes to an iron being taken from hot coals by a blacksmith and shaped into an implement. Refers to someone who should act immediately. *"Close the deal right away; you've got to strike while the iron is hot."*

Back in the saddle — alludes to a horseman who rides again after an absence. Refers to someone who returns to her responsibilities after being absent. *"She is back in the saddle after a lengthy illness."*

Ain't seen him in a coon's age — alludes to the life expectancy of a raccoon. Refers to a long period of time. *"We ain't seen Joe in a coon's age."*

Give it a lick and a promise — alludes to passing over something lightly with the tongue and promising more later. Refers to slight action and vowing to do a more thorough job later. *"The carpenter came by and gave the job a lick and a promise."*

Hold your horses — alludes to holding the reins of the horses tight so that they don't start moving. Refers to a command not to get impatient and start something before all are ready. *"We'll get to your problem; just hold your horses."*

Give it the gun — alludes to opening the throttle of an engine. Refers to rushing an action. *"Let's give it the gun and get out of here by midnight."*

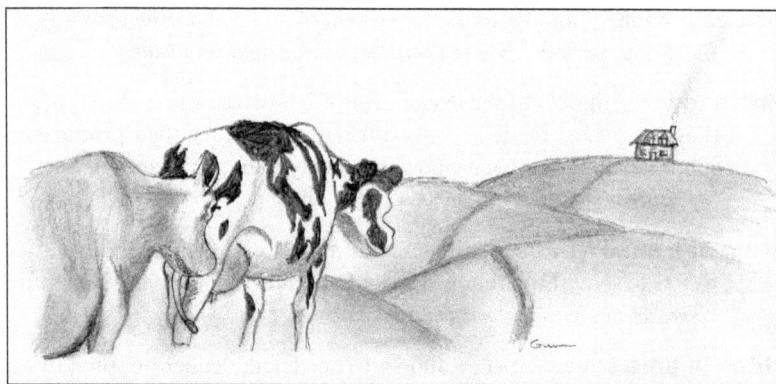

'Till the cows come home — alludes to cows that go out to pasture during the day and come home at night. Refers to waiting an indefinite time for someone or something. *"She'll wait for him 'till the cows come home."*

Burning the midnight oil — alludes to lamps that burned kerosene. Refers to staying up late to read or study. *"She burned the midnight oil studying for her history test."*

Goes to bed with the chickens — alludes to the fact that chickens go to roost before dark. Refers to someone who goes to bed early. *"He may get up early, but he goes to bed with the chickens."*

Time to hit the hay — alludes to the time the grass hay is mature enough to harvest. Refers to the time one is going to bed. *"She hit the hay early tonight."*

Put out to pasture — alludes to a racehorse that is retired from racing. Refers to someone who has been retired from his work. *"When they were able to hire younger guys, they put him out to pasture."*

A watched pot never boils — alludes to a pot of liquid boiling on a stove. Refers to the act of being impatient. *"Be patient with the project; a watched pot never boils."*

Hawk and a spit up the road — alludes to coughed up phlegm that is ejected. Refers to a very short distance. *"They live just a hawk and a spit up the road from here."*

Stone's throw away — alludes to throwing a small rock. Refers to a very short distance. *"They live just a stone's throw away from our house."*

As the crow flies — alludes to a bird that flies across the country. Refers to a short distance but not if you drive on the available roads. *"We are five miles from them but it's half that distance as the crow flies."*

Clear to hell and back — alludes to the distance to eternal damnation. Refers to a very long distance. *"That place is clear to hell and back from here."*

Can't step in the same creek twice — alludes to the constant flow of water that changes the creek. Refers to the concept that you cannot repeat a comment or a behavior with the same meaning. *"You've already stuck your foot in your mouth; you know you can't step in the same creek twice."*

Go'in like sixty — alludes to an automobile going sixty miles an hour in the days when going that fast was out of the ordinary and the speed limit was fifty. It originated when Phillips 66 developed a high octane gasoline. Refers to someone behaving or moving at an extra ordinary rate. *"She was a go'in like sixty to get ready for her company."*

Hotter than hell — alludes to the fire in Hades. Refers to temperatures that are high and intolerable. *"It's hotter than hell in that room."*

Frog croaker — alludes to the dying expression of an amphibian. Refers to a very heavy rain. *"That rain last night was a frog croaker."*

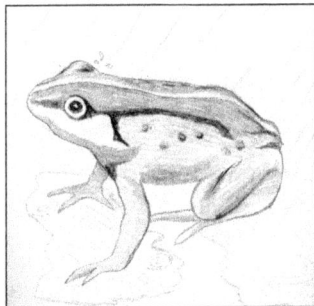

Colder than a well digger's ass or a dead bitch's teat in the Klondike — alludes to digging wells or a dead dog's teats in the cold northern part of Canada. Refers to an extremely cold temperature. *"Today the temperature is colder than a well digger's ass in the Klondike."*

Raining like a cow pissing on a flat rock — alludes to a cow that urinates on a flat rock causing the urine to splatter. Refers to a very heavy rain. *"It's raining like a cow pissing on a flat rock."*

Rain check — alludes to a ticket refund because of rain. Refers to postponing an engagement because of inconvenience at a particular time. *"May we take a rain check on your dinner invitation?"*

Come rain or come shine — alludes to raining and sun shining days. Refers to an absolute commitment. *"I'll be here tomorrow come rain or come shine."*

Smidgen off — alludes to a tiny bit. Refers to a small miscalculation. *"He was a smidgen off in his measurement of that board."*

A fine tooth comb — Alludes to a close tooth hair arranger. Refers to a careful and thorough examination or perusal of written material. *"She took the time to peruse his manuscript for grammatical error with a fine tooth comb."*

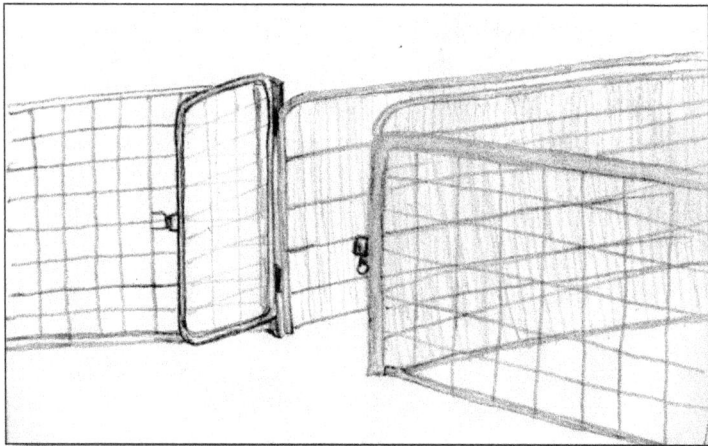

Potato wagon upset — alludes to a horse-drawn wagon filled with potatoes. Refers to rolling thunder. *"Sounds like the potato wagon upset; we'll get the rain next."*

Too late to shut the gate after the horses are out — alludes to the gate of a corral where horses are confined. Refers to a situation where it's too late to correct the problem. *"She left yesterday, it's too late to shut the gate after the horses are out."*

Raining cats and dogs — alludes to olden times when cats and dogs slept on thatch roofs and when it rained hard the animals would fall through the roof. Refers to a very heavy rain. *"It's raining cats and dogs out there now."*

Long row to hoe — alludes to hoeing a row of vegetables. Refers to a difficult and time-consuming task. *"She's got a long row to hoe with the healing of her broken leg."*

Down the road apiece — alludes to a long distance to travel. Refers to something happening in the distant future. *"That decision will need to be made down the road apiece."*

Drier than a popcorn fart — alludes to a fibrous, dry flatulent. Refers to the weather or soil conditions. *"With no rain last month, the fields and the wind are drier than a popcorn fart."*

Jerkwater town — alludes to a train stop that is only long enough to jerk the water tower spout down to fill the steam engine. Refers to a very small, insignificant community. *"He's a hayseed from a jerkwater town."*

Value

Worthless as teats on a boar — alludes to a male hog that has neither need nor capabilities to nurse. Refers to someone who has neither the capabilities, nor the talent for the task. *"When it comes to mechanics, he's worthless as teats on a boar."*

Not worth a hoot — alludes to an owl's common and frequent expression. Refers to something that is minimal in value. *"That guy ain't worth a hoot when it comes to fixin' things."*

Peaches and cream — alludes to a special dessert or dish. Refers to something or someone very special. *"You can tell that he's her peaches and cream."*

Not worth a hill of beans — alludes to common garden beans that are planted in small mounds of soil and are very plentiful. Refers to something or someone that is of very little value. *"That property deed is not worth a hill of beans."*

Worthless as a wart on your big toe — alludes to a hard growth of skin. Refers to an inconvenience or bothersome aspect. *"He is of little value in discussions; he's like a wart on your big toe."*

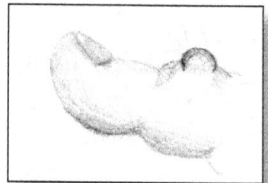

Fart in a windstorm — alludes to the insignificance of passing gas in a strong wind. Refers to someone without significant importance or value. *"Jim's importance in this matter is like a fart in a windstorm."*

Not worth a tinker's damn — alludes to a clumsy repairman's cursing. Refers to the potential altering of a condition or situation. *"That tractor is not worth a tinker's damn."*

Cream of the crop — alludes to the top quality produce. Refers to something or someone that is the best of its kind. *"That brand of seed is the cream of the crop."*

All that glitters is not gold — alludes to the appearance of a metal or ore. Refers to the outward appearance of someone or something which may fool you as to its true value or worth. *"They look like they are very compatible, but all that glitters is not gold."*

Even the chickens wouldn't eat it — alludes to chickens that eat table scraps, insects and worms. Refers to some prepared food that is very poor tasting. *"Even the chickens wouldn't eat her potato salad."*

Eating high on the hog — alludes to the tops of the hog from where the best cuts of pork come. Refers to someone who is wealthy or whose lifestyle is rich. *"With his inheritance he's living high on the hog."*

Scarcer than hen's teeth — alludes to chickens that have no teeth. Refers to something that is very scarce or non-existent. *"Good jobs around here are scarcer than hen's teeth."*

That ain't hay — alludes to grass hay which is plentiful. Refers to an expression used to describe something of value and costs a lot of money. *"His price for the wagon sure as hell ain't hay."*

Pick of the litter — alludes to the best of those pups born. Refers to the one that is outstanding. *"She's the pick of the litter when it comes to looks."*

Hog slop — alludes to the table scraps that are fed to pigs. Refers to things of little value. *"His opinion is hog slop."*

That's slop (swill) — alludes to watery table scraps fed to the hogs by throwing it on the ground or trough in the hog pen. Refers to ill-prepared, unappetizing and poorly served food. *"That café serves nothing but slop that isn't even fit for the hogs."*

Stands out like a nugget among pebbles — alludes to a piece of gold among small stones. Refers to something or someone who is more valuable than its surroundings. *"That piece of furniture stands out like a nugget among pebbles."*

In the blue chips — alludes to poker chips colored blue that represent the highest monetary value. Refers to having the high value or big profit. *"He's in the blue chips category when it comes to cattle."*

Can't make a silk purse out of a sow's ear — alludes to a delicate material (silk) and a tough and leathery ear of an old pig. Refers to a situation in which someone is trying to replace or remodel a valuable object with inferior material. *"Don't even try to repair that trunk with those pine boards; you can't make a silk purse out of a sow's ear."*

That's the sixty-four dollar question — alludes to a radio quiz show's final question in a series. Refers to a very difficult, elusive and important question. *"How she is going to react is the sixty-four dollar question."*

Competition

Cleaned their plow — alludes to an implement used to break up soil. Refers to the success of someone in regards to competition with others. *"In the softball game we cleaned their plows."*

Came back with his tail between his legs — alludes to a dog that has been beaten in a fight. Refers to someone who has been humbled by criticism or defeat. *"After losing the game, they came back with their tails between their legs."*

It's a scrub — alludes to an inferior breed of cattle or a cow that is no longer productive. Refers to someone who is less talented and/or productive. *"After his performance in the last game, the coach put him on the scrub team."*

Helpless as a pig on ice — alludes to a short legged, cloven-hoofed mammal on a slick surface. Refers to someone who is awkward and lacks physical coordination. *"They don't have a chance against us; they are helpless as a pig on ice."*

Left sucking hind teat — alludes to the last udder of a pig that is small and inefficient. Refers to someone who comes in last in competition. *"We were first and they were left sucking hind teat."*

Nailed his hide to the wall — alludes to the process of drying the skin/fur of an animal on a wall to dry. Refers to pinning down or badly beating an opponent in a sport. *"In football we nailed their hides to the wall."*

Scalded and picked clean — alludes to the removal of the feathers on a fowl before butchering it. Refers to someone who has been taken to task or defeated badly. *"They scalded and picked the other team clean."*

Beat the socks off them — alludes to stripping off their foot covering. Refers to defeating someone or a team very badly. *"We beat the socks off Savannah's team."*

Took them to the cleaners — alludes to an establishment where clothes are washed. Refers to one defeating another decisively. *"Maryville took Cameron to the cleaners in football."*

Took them to the wood shed — alludes to an outbuilding where wood and cobs were stored but also served as a place where the father would take his son for a spanking away from the mother. Refers to the beating of a sports team. *"Maryville took Red Oak to the wood shed in basketball."*

Make mince meat pie of them — alludes to a pastry containing finely chopped apples, raisins, spices and meat. Refers to destroying an enemy or defeating an opposing team badly. *"In basketball, the Northwest team will make minced meat pie of the Missouri Western team."*

Feather in his hat — alludes to a huntsman who shoots a game bird and puts one of its feathers in the band of his hat. Refers to someone who has accomplished a feat. *"Being awarded the contract is a feather in his hat."*

Separating the cream from milk — alludes to using a separator to get the quality cream separated from skimmed milk. Refers to the separation of a quality athlete or team from other athletes or teams. *"When Missouri beats Texas, they'll be separating the cream from the milk."*

Separate the wheat from the chaff — alludes to the wheat kernel and the stems. Refers to the separation of quality performance from the mediocre. *"It was a one sided victory; they separated the wheat from the chaff."*

A bunch of culls — alludes to hen chickens that no longer produce eggs. Refers to those who are inferior in physical ability. *"Their whole team is made up of a bunch of culls."*

Wrung 'em out and hung them up to dry — alludes to the clothes washing process. Refers to beating an opponent badly. *"Our football team beat theirs; we wrung 'em out and hung them up to dry."*

Knocked his chip or block off — alludes to someone with a chip of wood on his shoulder. Refers to someone who took another person's challenge and defeated him.
"Joe irritated him, so he knocked his block off."

They locked horns — alludes to two buck deer engaging in battle. Refers to two teams playing each other in a sport or in an argument. *"Next Saturday, Missouri will lock horns with Nebraska in the basketball play-offs."*

Money and *Finance*

Squeeze a nickel until the buffalo farts or until the Indian is riding the buffalo — alludes to the old nickel coin with the image of an Indian on one side and a buffalo on the other. Refers to someone who is very frugal. *"Joe won't pay for dinner; he'd squeeze a nickel until the Indian is riding the buffalo."*

Tighter than last winter's long johns — alludes to the fitting of year old long underwear. Refers to someone who does not wish to part with his money. *"Fred is very conservative; he's tighter than last winter's long johns."*

Tighter than the bark on a tree — alludes to the close relationship of the outer covering to the core of the tree. Refers to someone who is very conservative with his/her money. *"When it comes to church support; he's tighter than the bark on a tree."*

Tighter than a tick in a coon dog's ear —alludes to a small blood-sucking insect that has lodged itself in the floppy ear of a coon dog. Refers to someone who is very conservative with money. *"He won't pick up the check, he's tighter than a tick in a coon dog's ear."*

Belly up — alludes to a fish that has died and is floating with its stomach up above the water level. Refers to a company that can't meet its financial obligations or has gone broke. *"The airline couldn't show a profit and it has gone belly up."*

Chicken feed — alludes to the small grain and amount it takes to feed chickens. Refers to a small amount of money. *"That is chicken feed compared with its cost."*

Keeping ahead of the hounds — alludes to a raccoon that is running ahead of the coonhounds or hunting dogs. Refers to someone whose financial gains are just ahead of his/her expenses. *"We're not getting rich, but we're keeping ahead of the hounds."*

Drop in the bucket — alludes to a very small amount of water in a large container. Refers to a small amount of money in regards to what is needed or expected. *"What he's got is a drop in the bucket compared with what he needs."*

Brings home the bacon — alludes to the purchase of quality pork. Refers to someone who is the main wage earner. *"She is the one in the family who brings home the bacon."*

Eatin' high on the hog — alludes to the region of the hog that contains the best quality of meat cuts. Refers to a wealthy lifestyle. *"Since they got a good price for their corn, they are eatin' high on the hog."*

The well has gone dry — alludes to a water well from which water is pumped. Refers to a money source that is no longer available. *"After their liberal spending, the well has gone dry."*

If cloth was a nickel a yard, they couldn't afford enough to fit a piss ant with boxer shorts — alludes (a hyperbole) to a very small insect being fitted with human underwear. Refers to someone who is very poor or financially embarrassed. *"If cloth was a nickel a yard, John couldn't afford enough to fit a piss ant with boxer shorts."*

A tightwad — alludes to a firmly packed ball or folded material. Refers to someone who is very frugal or stingy. *"That old tightwad wouldn't buy a pair of gloves if his hands were freezing."*

Staying alive to avoid funeral expenses — alludes to the significant amount it costs to prepare and bury a body. Refers to someone who is very financially conservative. *"He's so stingy with his money, he'd stay alive just to avoid funeral expenses."*

Blew the egg money — alludes to the money in the farmer's wife's special fund from selling the chicken eggs. Refers to someone who exhausts one's funds on some extravagant purchase. *"She spent all his money and than she blew the egg money on her new dress."*

Poor as a church mouse — alludes to a mouse that lives in a church where there is little food for it to eat. Refers to someone who has very little money to live on. *"Since his crops flooded out, he's poor as a church mouse."*

Don't take any plug nickels — alludes to a worthless circular coin shaped metal knocked out of electrical boxes. Refers to warning against being duped. *"When you are dealing with him, make sure you don't take any plug nickels."*

Can't get blood from a turnip — alludes to a root vegetable that has little juice. Refers to someone who has no money. *"You just as well forget the debt; you can't get blood from a turnip."*

Don't have a pot to pee in — alludes to urinating in a chamber pot. Refers to someone who is lacking financially. *"He's so poor he doesn't have a pot to pee in."*

Bought a pig in a poke — alludes to buying a pig (which may be a cat) in a gunnysack sight unseen. Refers to buying anything unseen. *"He bought a pig in a poke, when he bought that used car."*

Ear marked — alludes to a pig's ear chink, slit or tag that distinguishes it from other pigs. Refers to legislated funds for a particular favored constituency separated from general funding. *"Senator Kerpotcan had ear marked millions of dollars for his State's projects."*

Let the cat out of the bag — alludes to someone selling a fictitious pig that is really a cat, in a poke, but the cat jumps out of the bag during the transaction. Refers to someone who exposes to the public private information. *"She let the cat out of the bag in regards to their plans."*

Left holding the bag — alludes to a trick in which someone is invited to go "snipe hunting" and is instructed to hold a bag while others chase the fictitious snipe into the bag. Refers to someone who is left to pay the bill or debt in a financial transaction. *"The others took off and he was left holding the bag."*

Put it on the cuff — alludes to a waiter who records fees or costs on the cuff of his sleeve. Refers to charging an amount of money. *"Please put the cost on the cuff."*

Charge it to the wind and let the dust settle it — alludes to wind blown dust. Refers to dismissing the charge. *"You don't owe me anything; charge it to the wind and let the dust settle it."*

Feathered his own nest — alludes to fowl or birds that peck and gather materials and feathers to make their hatching nest soft and warm. Refers to someone who applies common funds to his/her own account. *"The auditor caught him feathering his own nest."*

Bum steer — alludes to a steer (castrated bull) that wanders from the herd during the round up. Refers to erroneous advice or misdirected information. *"He gave me a bum steer with his investment advice."*

Sold a bill of goods — alludes to a paper account of the goods without the actual goods. Refers to accepting and paying for a promise of something. *"He purchased a bill of goods rather than the wheat that he was expecting."*

Don't look a gift horse in the mouth — alludes to a horse's mouth that is a good indication of the horse's health and age. Refers to advice to a person who is about to receive a gift. *"That may not be the best quality, but don't look a gift horse in the mouth."*

Relationships

Made from the same leather — alludes to two products made from the same cowhide. Refers to two people who are much alike. *"So, you like country music? We must be made from the same leather."*

The apple don't fall too far from the tree — alludes to an apple that is ripe usually falling straight down to the ground. Refers to people who are like their parents in looks and behavior. *"That's his kid over there; the apple don't fall too far from the tree."*

Going against the grain — alludes to sawing a board against the wood's grain and causing it to splinter. Refers to someone who does not conform to the norm or behaves differently. *"He tends to go against the grain in most discussions or situations."*

Blood is thicker than water — alludes to the texture of blood and water. Refers to people who are inherently closer to family than to other people. *"He won't testify against his own brother; blood is thicker than water."*

Took hook, line and sinker — alludes to a fish that took all the necessary appendages of a fishing line. Refers to one who believes or accepts all that was proposed or presented. *"She fell for him and takes what he says, hook, line and sinker."*

The pot calling the kettle black — alludes to a cooking utensil used on an open fire which are tarnished by smoke. *"She is as guilty as he is; her comments are like the pot calling the kettle black."*

Birds of a feather flock together — alludes to birds of the same genus family getting together. Refers to people who have things, attitudes or ideas alike gathering together. *"The Baptists are all over there; birds of a feather flock together."*

Close as wagon tracks to the ground — alludes to ruts made by horse drawn wagons. Refers to a relationship or proximity of two items. *"Those gals are as close as wagon tracks to the ground."*

Water seeks its own level — alludes to water that flows to pools in a stream and somewhat settles there. Refers to people who seek to associate with others with the same abilities, intellect or attitudes/beliefs. *"Ed and Sara are good friends; water seeks its own level."*

Chickens will come home to roost — alludes to a flock of chickens that feed individually but just before dark, they all go to the chicken house to roost. Refers to an individual of a family or group who has gone astray but probably will return home or to a wrongful action or punishment that will come back to a person. *"He did us wrong, but the chickens will come home to roost."*

Been through the grist mill — alludes to ground grain. Refers to someone who has experienced extensive physical or emotional problems. *"The poor gal has been through the mill with domestic violence."*

Chip off the old block — alludes to a block of wood or stone that has been chipped. Refers to an offspring that is like a parent. *"He's of no count for he's like his old man; he's a chip off the old block."*

Left holding the bag — alludes to the gullible young person who is persuaded by conspirators to hold a bag at the end of a field. The conspirators leave falsely promising that they are going to chase snipe (a very small bird) from the field into the bag being held open by the naïve young man. Refers to someone who is left with all the responsibilities or tasks. *"The other workers quit and left him holding the bag."*

Thicker than molasses in January — alludes to thick syrup that is very difficult to manipulate when it is cold. Refers to people who are very difficult to separate. *"That whole family is thick as molasses in January."*

Taken under her wing — alludes to fowl that take chicks under their wings to protect them. Refers to accepting the responsibility for another. *"He was always in trouble until she took him under her wing."*

Stuck her neck out for him — alludes to a chicken with its neck on the chopping block. Refers to someone who becomes vulnerable to criticism by defending the actions or ideas of someone. *"She stuck her neck out when she defended his judgment in the matter."*

Out foxed — alludes to a very cunning animal. Refers to someone who is more deceptive than the other person. *"She out foxed him in that situation."*

Every kettle must sit on its own bottom — alludes to the difficulty with trying to stack kettles (kitchen, iron cooking utensils). Refers to an individual's responsibilities within a relationship. *"It is alright to help, but every kettle must sit on its own bottom."*

Gets my goat — alludes to a goat used as security for a flock of sheep or in a thoroughbred horse's stall being removed. Refers to someone's behavior that unnerves you or makes you feel uneasy. *"She really gets my goat when she talks about my former wife."*

Death and Dying

Kicked the bucket — alludes to the farmer who is milking a cow, falls off the stool and kicks the milk bucket. Refers to dying. *"Poor old Jim; he kicked the bucket last week."*

Bought the farm — alludes to a farmer whose life insurance bought the farm upon his death. Refers to dying. *"Poor old Pete, he bought the farm last year."*

The grim reaper cut him down — alludes to death as depicted by a man with a scythe. Refers to someone who died. *"You can't escape the grim reaper who cuts a wide swathe."*

About to croak — alludes to utterance of a hoarse low-pitched cry of a frog, especially after it has been gigged. Refers to someone who is about to die. *"Joe looks as if he's about to croak."*

Went to her reward — alludes to receiving recognition and honor. Refers to someone dying after living an exceptional life. *"At the age of sixty, she went to her reward."*

About to fall through the cracks — alludes to cracks in the floor separating life and death. Refers to someone who is dying. *"He's on his death bed and is about to fall through the cracks."*

One foot in the grave — alludes to the hole they dig to bury someone. Refers to someone near death. *"I saw him yesterday and he's got one foot in the grave."*

About to put the last nail in his coffin — alludes to a box for corpses. Refers to someone near death. *"They removed life support and are about to put the last nail in his coffin."*

Dead as a doornail — alludes to a long, strong flat-headed nail that is very difficult to remove after it is driven into a board. Refers to someone who is unquestionably dead. *"They found him near his tractor dead as a doornail."*

Pullin' up turnips with a six-foot ladder — alludes to the common burial in a six-foot hole in the ground. Refers to someone who is dead and buried. *"The reason you haven't seen him is because he's now pullin' up turnips with a six-foot ladder."*

Living on borrowed time — alludes to someone who lives on a promise. Refers to someone who is about to die. *"She's been living on borrowed time for two years."*

Sent to the glue factory — alludes to the rendering plant where livestock's hoofs are made into glue. Refers to the death of an animal. *"The horse has been sent to the glue factory."*

Didn't come in on the last load of turnips — alludes to a trailer filled in the turnip field. Refers to someone who has died. *"He didn't come in on the last load of turnips yesterday."*

Shouldn't buy green bananas — alludes to the few days it takes bananas to ripen. Refers to someone who probably will die in a day or two. *"The way he looks, he shouldn't buy green bananas."*

Looks like death eating a cracker — alludes to the image of a very pale father time eating a soda cracker. Refers to someone who is pale and about to die. *"He's about to go; he looks like death eating a cracker."*

Crossed the vale — alludes to the valley between life and eternal rest. Refers to dying. *"She has crossed the vale."*

Passed away — alludes to moving away from something. Refers to passing from life to eternity or dying. *"She passed away last night."*

Called home — alludes to being called to the eternal life. Refers to having died. *"He has been called home."*

Gone to his eternal rest — alludes to peace hereafter. Refers to having died. *"He's no longer with us; he's gone to his eternal rest."*

Communication
and *Language Skills*

Watch your 'p's and 'q's —alludes to the confusion of the two letters on a typesetting press. Refers to being cautious about what you say, how you say it and how you behave. *"Watch your 'p's and 'q's around him; he's looking for arguments."*

Read between the lines — alludes to reading and further interpreting meaning. Refers to hidden or suggested meaning of a written message. *"With his writing, you often have to read between the lines."*

Take with a grain of salt — alludes to a small insignificant mineral flavoring. Refers to something said that is of little consequence. *"He really doesn't know; you take what he says with a grain of salt."*

Not the whole piece of cloth — alludes to a piece of cloth that has part of it missing. Refers to a story or information that has important parts missing. *"You heard their side of the story, but that's not the whole piece of cloth."*

In one ear and out the other — alludes to sound passing through one ear and out the other without the attention of the brain. Refers to someone who doesn't listen. *"Forget trying to explain it to him; it'll go in one ear and out the other."*

Keep your ear to the ground — alludes to listening to the ground to detect coming horses or animals. Refers to keeping alert for relevant messages. *"We need to discover his plans; so keep your ear to the ground."*

Lend me your ear — alludes to figuratively borrowing someone's ear. Refers to a request to listen. *"If you will lend me your ear, I'll be happy to explain."*

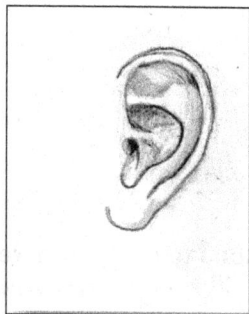

Spilled the beans — alludes to spilling a bowl of beans or vegetables. Refers to someone who reveals something he/she was held in confidence not to reveal. *"Well, she spilled the beans on their plans for a short get away."*

Beating his gums — alludes to the fleshy tissue that surrounds the teeth after teeth have been removed. Refers to rapid, sometimes excessive, talking on one's part. *"He's been beating his gums in there for thirty minutes."*

Bending her ear — alludes to turning an ear to someone. Refers to the listening to someone who speaks over an extended period of time. *"He's been bending her ear for over an hour."*

Got a frog in his throat — alludes to a tailless amphibian that croaks with a husky pitch. Refers to someone who has a hoarse or raspy voice caused by phlegm. *"He'd had a bad cold; in the middle of the song he got a frog in his throat."*

The cat's meow — alludes to the cry of the house cat. Refers to a spiteful comment. *"Your last statement was the cat's meow."*

That's hogwash — alludes to the senseless washing of a hog that wallows in the mud to keep cool. Refers to an unnecessary or unbelievable comment or statement. *"His statement about the deal is hogwash."*

Dumb cluck — alludes to silent and senseless vocalization of a hen chicken. Refers to someone speaking, who is naïve and doesn't know "sic cum from cum err." *"You dumb cluck, what do you know about field corn?"*

Barking at the moon — alludes to a dog that barks at the moon for an unknown cause. Refers to misguided information or exaggerated statements. *"Don't listen to him; he's just barking at the moon."*

Got it straight from the horse's mouth — alludes to a racehorse telling how it is going to do in a race. Refers to information from the primary source. *"They are going to separate; I got it straight from the horse's mouth."*

All ears — alludes to both ears. Refers to someone who is intently listening. *"If it comes to making money, he'll be all ears."*

Talked his ear off — alludes to someone's ear falling off from another person's talk. Refers to the act of speaking intensely for a long period of time. *"After church she almost talked my ear off."*

Turn a deaf ear to him — to aim the ear with which one has significant hearing loss toward someone. Refers to the practice of not listening. *"Turn a deaf ear to him when he begins to tell his stories."*

Bellers like a stuck cow — alludes to the vocalization of a cow when a knife is stuck into one of her stomachs to relieve the bloating. Refers to loud and unnecessary complaining. *"He believes that he was done wrong; so he's bellering like a stuck cow."*

When he begins to talk, his brain goes into neutral — alludes to not being able to think while speaking. Refers to someone who doesn't think about what he is saying. *"She's a well meaning lady, but when she speaks her mind goes into neutral."*

Play it by ear — alludes to listening carefully. Refers to someone who should not speak before analyzing what others have said. *"In this situation I advise you to play it by ear."*

Put his foot in his mouth — alludes to an unusual and difficult act. Refers to someone who gets into trouble by saying the wrong thing. *"At the party, he really stuck his foot in his mouth."*

Having a rhubarb — alludes to a sour tasting, coarse, perennial herb that is commonly grown and called "pie plant." Refers to an argument. *"They're good friends but they are just having a rhubarb."*

Lots of chattering — alludes to birds communicating vocally. Refers to informal conversation containing gossip. *"The ladies are doing a lot of chattering in the kitchen."*

Can't tell a book by its cover — alludes to determining the quality and interest level of a book's message by its cover. Refers to not being able to determine someone's character by his appearance. *"Don't judge him too hastily, you can't tell a book by its cover."*

Read him like a book — alludes to the process of seeing and interpreting verbal messages. Refers to the act of observing and understanding human behavior. *"When it comes to money, she can read him like a book."*

Bone to pick — alludes to dogs that are claiming the same bone. Refers to the expression of different views or opinions. *"I have a bone to pick with you in regards to your opinion of her."*

With our hats in our hands — alludes to meeting someone with an uncovered head with their hat in your hand, showing respect at the door. Refers to expressing an apology. *"For you not being invited, we come to you with our hats in our hands."*

Dot your 'i's and cross your 't's — alludes to manuscript writing. Refers to expressing yourself very carefully so you don't expose yourself to criticism. *"When you're communicating with him, make sure that you dot your 'i's and cross your 't's."*

Raise the devil — alludes to causing the devil to come out from hell. Refers to someone who is being critical with a loud and harsh voice. *"She raised the devil with me about my actions."*

Tacked his hide to the wall — alludes to the method of curing animal hide and fur by stretching it on a wall. Refers to someone who through his/her argument has appropriately censured someone. *"They nailed his hide to the wall in regards to his neglecting the problem."*

Hen scratches — alludes to a hen chicken scratching the soil indiscriminately and in an unorganized fashion searching for worms and bugs. Refers to unintelligible or incoherent writing. *"No one could decipher or understand her hen scratches."*

Chewing her cud — alludes to a cow that has regurgitated ruminants from it first stomach to its mouth for further chewing. Refers to idle or empty talk. *"They're in the kitchen chewing their cuds."*

Hoof and mouth disease — alludes to a contagious disease of cattle. Refers to someone who is constantly spreading rumors. *"Don't listen to her; she has hoof and mouth disease."*

Full of beans — alludes to plant pods that are flatulent in nature, especially if eaten in quantity. Refers to one who is full of hot air and doesn't know what he/she is talking about. *"Don't listen to him; he is full of beans."*

Gotta hit 'em in the head with a 2x4 — alludes to the belief that one has to hit a donkey or mule in the head with a big sick in order to get it to obey commands. Refers to getting the attention of someone who has difficulty listening. *"You about have to hit him in the head with a 2x4 to get him to listen."*

Kitchen, Household and Food

Don't mix your meat with your potatoes — alludes to dinner table etiquette in which you are to savor each portion of food separately. It is used as a warning to someone in reference to mixing his personal life with his work or job. When I was in high school, I worked for the local chicken hatchery and produce store, and I accompanied an "older" and married guy on the Saturday produce route to the farm homes. While I waited in the truck the guy would go in the house to "visit" with the farm wives. I wanted to say, *"Charlie, you better not mix your meat with your potatoes."*

Meat and potatoes man — alludes to meat and potatoes as being the basic, common diet for a hard working farmer. Refers to someone who does not appreciate gourmet, fancy or exotic varieties of food. *"Let's skip going to a restaurant; I'm a meat and potatoes man."*

Let Eloise make the gravy — alludes to a practice in which the gravy, a difficult mixture to make without lumps, is delegated to the woman of the house who is usually successful in making it. Refers to warning someone not to interfere by trying to compete or advise a qualified person who is processing a task. *"Don't bother her; let Eloise make the gravy."*

Too many cooks in the kitchen spoil the stew — alludes to the number of cooks involved in making a stew that can contain a variety of choices of meat, spices and vegetables. It is used as a warning to people who are eager to advise someone on a task that he/she is attempting. *"Leave Joe alone; too many cooks spoil the stew."*

Full as a tick — alludes to a blood-sucking insect that embeds itself in an animal or human and sucks blood out of the victim until its stomach is bulging and about to burst. Refers to someone who comments that he/she has had more than enough to eat. *"After that big meal, I'm full as a tick."*

Brought all the fixins — alludes to a custom or practice of someone bringing home all the ingredients necessary for making a particular dish or entire meal. Refers to a situation in which all the ingredients, parts or attitudes are available. *"She brought all the fixins for having a good time."*

Thin as soup made from a starving sparrow — alludes to a liquid made from the stock of a small bird that has starved to death. It was used to describe someone who was very, very thin or a very thin liquid. *"Have you seen Kay? She's as thin as soup made from a starving sparrow."*

Thick as pea soup — alludes to a comparatively thick creamy soup. Refers to foggy weather and one's ability to see. *"Wait for the fog to clear; it's thick as pea soup out there."*

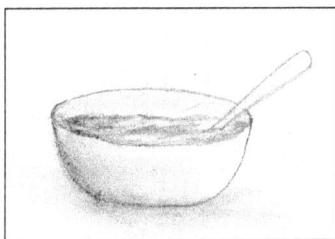

Got himself in the soup (or pickle) — both soup and pickle describe an inescapable situation. Alludes to someone who was in a precarious situation or trouble. *"By taking the truck, he got himself in the soup."*

Two pickles short of a quart — alludes to a jar of homemade pickles that isn't quite full. It is used to describe someone who is naïve or lacks common sense. *"Don't do what he does; he's two pickles short of a quart jar."*

Got pickled — alludes to the process of being preserved by brine. Refers to someone who has had too much alcohol to drink. *"He really got pickled last night. I knew this guy back home who got pickled everyday, and he died of cirrhosis."*

Half baked — alludes to potatoes or other baked items that are not completely done or baked. Refers to someone's idea or suggestion that is not thought through thoroughly. It was often used to describe an immature person. *"Jim and his half baked ideas should be ignored. The elders of the community referred to me when I was a 'kid' as being half-baked."*

Hard boiled — alludes to boiling an egg until the yolk is set or solid. Refers to a person who is set in his/her ways and is obstinate. *"He's hard boiled and difficult to get along with."*

Made from scratch — alludes to a food product that is developed completely from raw materials or "homemade" and is not purchased or "store bought" in a box. It is derived from the concept of chickens scratching the soil for food. Refers to a food, craft or clothing that is developed from basic, primary items or had no prior preparation. *"Her fruit pies are always made from scratch."*

That takes the cake — alludes to a contest in which the prize is a cake such as in a "cake walk." Refers to someone who does something remarkable or some extraordinary or unbelievable event or occurrence. It is often used in a negative tone similar to *"That was the last straw. His apology took the cake."*

That's the frosting on the cake — alludes to the last step in cake baking which is spreading frosting or icing on the baked cake. Refers to the extra special or final touch to a project or task. *"Her acceptance of the responsibility was the frosting on the cake."*

You can't have your cake and eat it too — the allusion here is self-explanatory. Refers to situations where a choice or decision has to be made in an either/or dilemma. *"You must choose one or the other; you can't have your cake and eat it too."*

There's a lot of frosting on that cake — alludes to thick, fluffy, extra sweet material or icing that covers the true cake. Refers to someone who appears artificial or hides his/her true nature. *"Joe is not all that he appears to be; there's a lot of frosting on that cake."*

A piece of cake — alludes to dessert cake that is easy to eat no matter what the meal. Refers to an easy, enjoyable and quick task. *"Finding his place is a piece of cake."*

Killed the fatted calf — alludes to the Biblical reference about the prodigal son. Refers to a large spread of food or banquet. *"What a feast; you must have killed the fatted calf."*

Best bib and tucker — alludes to a linen cloth (bib) and a piece of lace (tucker) worn around a lady's neck. Refers to formal dress for a special occasion. *"They wore their best bib and tucker to the party."*

Like trying to nail Jello to the wall — alludes to a gelatin substance or semi liquid (trade name is Jello). Refers to a very difficult if not impossible task. *"Getting her to go is like trying to nail Jello to the wall."*

Cookin' for threshers — alludes to the practice of 'threshing' that existed before the wheat was combined in the field. In those days the wheat shocks were hauled to the farm home and a portable threshing machine was used to separate the wheat kernel from the chafe. The process usually involved more than six men, and the women of the house would cook large quantities of food for those who came to help with the threshing. Refers to large quantities of materials usually food. *"She really fixed a lot of food; you'd think she was cookin' for threshers."*

They cooked his goose — alludes to the cooking of someone's goose. Refers to someone who has caused ill will in regards to another through public criticism. *"She cooked his goose in regards to the other farmers."*

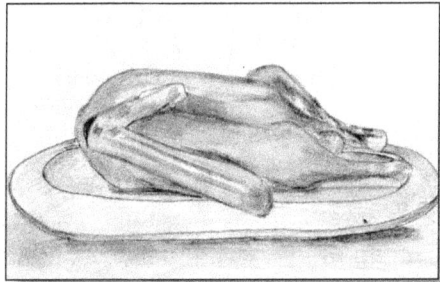

Cookin' something up — alludes to the practice of preparing food through the process of heat. Refers to the planning or plotting of an event or action. *"There is never a dull day; he's always cookin' something up."*

About to boil — alludes to a liquid that is heated close to the boiling point when it turns to vapor. Refers to someone who is about to become extremely angry. *"After her derogatory comment, he was about to boil."*

Having a rhubarb — alludes to a bitter tasting leafstalk and root used for sauces or pies. Refers to a bitter verbal exchange or argument. *"The umpire and the manager were having a rhubarb."*

Walking on eggshells — alludes to the thin fragile nature of a chicken eggshell. Refers to someone who needs to proceed with caution. *"As far as his job is concerned, he is walking on eggshells."*

Chewing the fat — alludes to masticating or attempting to crush a flexible substance. Refers to a conversation or verbal exchange. *"They are in the living room chewing the fat."*

Cream always rises — alludes to the processing of raw milk in which the butterfat or cream rises to the top of a container of milk. Refers to those who are talented or gifted rising above the others. *"She will win the contest: cream always rises."*

Separate the cream from the milk — alludes to separating the cream (in the old days the quality substance) from the milk that has not been homogenized. Refers to the separation of those who are more talented or products of higher quality. *"This test will separate the cream from the milk. We are dealing with the cream of the crop."*

It was a bad churn — alludes to the process of churning cream into butter when the butter is discolored or doesn't solidify. Refers to when a process or endeavor fails to meet expectations. *"They got a bad churn on that project."*

Every mother loves her own butter —alludes to the pride one takes in the churning process of butter. Refers to the pride a mother has in regards to her own children. *"He may have done wrong but his mother will stick up for him; you know every mother loves her own butter."*

Butter up — alludes to spreading of the fatty substance derived from milk. It is used to describe someone who flatters or praises someone while anticipating a favor. *"She buttered him up to get him to buy the ring."*

Hot butter wouldn't melt in her mouth — alludes to semi-liquid butterfat not changing to liquid. Refers to someone who has a cold personality or is aloof. *"The tragedy won't affect her; hot butter won't melt in her mouth."*

Full of it as a Christmas goose — alludes to the large quantity of dressing or stuffing put into the cavity of the goose that is being baked for Christmas dinner. Refers to someone who tends to exaggerate, enhance or embellish the facts. *"Don't believe everything he says; he's as full of it as a Christmas goose."*

Full of prunes — alludes to dried plums that aid in bowel regularity. Refers to someone who embellishes the truth or doesn't know what he/she is talking about. *"John is full of prunes when it comes to soil conservation."*

There's many of slips between the cup and the lip — alludes to the accidental spilling of tea or liquid while drinking. Refers to a warning to people who conversing over a cup of liquid may reveal someone's secret or private information. It was used as a warning during World War I and World War II. *"Beware of what you are saying; there's many of slips between the cup and the lip."*

The proof is in the pudding — alludes to the tasting of the pudding, which is a sweet, flour mixture used for a dessert. Refers to the end result of an endeavor rather than the person or process of concocting it. *"In regards to that action, the proof will be in the pudding."*

Don't know beans from apple butter — alludes to the comparison of two different foods. Refers to someone who is very naïve and lacks common sense. *"When it comes to cooking, she don't know beans from apple butter."*

Spilled the beans — alludes to someone who has upset a kettle of beans. Refers to someone who has publicly revealed private information. *"She spilled the beans in regards to our agreement."*

Don't cry over spilled milk — alludes to an accident of upsetting a container of a plentiful substance of cow's milk. Refers to someone being upset over an insignificant happening or occurrence. *"The damage will be ok; don't cry over spilled milk."*

Full of beans — alludes to someone who has overeaten on beans, which are flatulent causing. Refers to someone who is frisky or one who doesn't know what he/she is talking about. *"When it comes to raising hogs, he is full of beans."*

Kettle of hot water — alludes to a large vessel of water being heated to a high temperature on a stove. Refers to someone who is in trouble or has serious problems. *"Because of his actions he got himself into a kettle of hot water."*

Jumpy as a bubble on the griddle — alludes to a drop of water on a hot griddle or flat iron stove. Refers to someone who is very nervously active. *"Before his performance, he was as jumpy as a bubble on a griddle."*

Shouldn't buy green bananas — alludes to the relatively short time that it takes for bananas to ripen after they are purchased from the store. Refers to a person who appears close to death. *"Harry shouldn't buy green bananas; he looks like he's about to kick the bucket."*

Fly in the soup — alludes to an insect, the fly that lands and contaminates a bowl of broth thus causing an unpleasant situation. Refers to a problem that distracts from a process or event. *"Thing were going well until his craftsmanship became a fly in the soup."*

Fine kettle of fish — alludes to boiling fish. Refers to a predicament or bad situation. *"He talked himself into a fine kettle of fish."*

Thicker than molasses in January — alludes to a thick sugary syrup derived from sorghum (a field crop) that becomes practically solid in cold temperatures. It may refer to a substance as well as personal relationships. *"Since she came back, they are as thick as molasses in January."*

That's the way the cookie crumbles — alludes to the unpredictable nature of a crispy cookie breaking apart; sometimes causing embarrassing crumbs. Refers to unpredictable circumstances that are sometimes unpleasant but happen during a process. *"It is too bad that you did not fair better, but that's the way the cookie crumbles."*

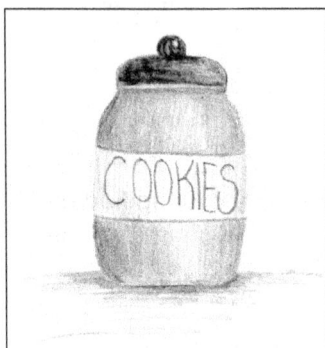

Caught with a hand in the cookie jar — in the olden days the cookie jar, full of tantalizing cookies, was always on a counter in the kitchen tempting young and old to sneak one or two between meals. Refers to someone who has committed a wrongdoing and has been apprehended. *"The bank clerk got caught with her hand in the cookie jar."*

Tough cookie — alludes to a cookie that is stale or ill baked and is difficult to chew. Refers to a physically hardy person who is aggressive in nature. *"Don't mess with him; he's one tough cookie."*

If you can't take the heat, get out of the kitchen — alludes to the high degree of heat created by the cookstove burning cobs and coal especially while using the oven to bake. Refers to someone who has been criticized and is told that if he/she can't take the abuse, he/she should resign or get out of the situation. President Harry Truman made this folk saying popular. *"I'm tired of hearing you complain; if you can't take the heat, get out of the kitchen."*

Don't bite off more than you can chew — alludes to a warning to someone, usually a child, at the dinner table not to fill his/her mouth to the point of embarrassment. Refers to a warning that someone should not try to do more than he/she is capable of doing. *"I wouldn't bite off more than I could chew; let someone else take that responsibility."*

You just as well partake of the devil as to taste of his broth — this allusion, Biblical in nature, uses the image of someone sipping an evil mixture without indulging in the substance. Refers to a warning that it is just as wrong to contemplate or think of committing a sinful act, as it is to commit it. *"It's a sin to even think about it; you just as well partake of the devil as to taste of his broth."*

You can attract more flies with honey than you can with vinegar — I don't know why anyone would want to attract flies literally, but it is an interesting allusion. Refers to the notion that a warm friendly attitude is more effective than a cold indifference in establishing and maintaining a relationship. *"Don't be mean and cold to him, you can attract more flies with honey than you can with vinegar."*

As difficult as picking fly dung out of pepper — alludes to the fact that both ground pepper and fly (the insect) dung are minute and black in nature and indistinguishable. Refers to a task that is practically impossible. *"Getting him to admit that he is wrong is as difficult as trying to pick fly dung out of pepper."*

Plate is full — alludes to a dinner plate or china that is heaped with food. Refers to someone who has many concerns or responsibilities. *"Right now, her plate is full."*

Sink your teeth into — alludes to biting and chewing solid tasty food. Refers to a task or project in which one can really get involved and have control. *"You can really sink your teeth into that project."*

Eatin' high on the hog — alludes to eating top quality pork such as loin or chops. Refers to living a life of luxury. *"He built a new house and is eatin' high on the hog."*

Out of the frying pan into the fire — alludes to meat that is being fried over open flames. Refers to someone who is in a bad situation and gets into a worse one. *"With that comment, he went from the frying pan and into the fire."*

Ugly as homemade soap — alludes to soap made of tallow and lye that has a brownish hue to it. Refers to a person who is not good looking. *"Poor Jane, she's as ugly as homemade soap."*

Dish it out — alludes to distributing the meal's food proportionately or ladling soup. Refers to criticizing or joking. *"She can dish it out, but she can't take it."*

Knows what side of the bread his butter is on — alludes to a slice of bread that has butter on one side. Refers to someone who knows to whom he/she is obligated for his/her welfare. *"Joe will do it for he knows what side of the bread his butter is on."*

Finger in too many pies — alludes to a cook who is trying to build several pies or pastries at the same time. Refers to someone who is trying too many things at one time and is failing to accomplish anything.
"Don't ask him; he's got his finger in too many pies the way it is."

Eatin' humble pie — alludes to the consumption of a pastry. Refers to someone who has had to apologize for what he/she has done.
"He had to eat humble pie for what he did."

In his/her cups — alludes to someone whose head has fallen on his/her cup. Refers to someone who is intoxicated or had too much alcohol to drink. *"Helen is in her cups again tonight."*

Still perkin' — alludes to a coffee percolator that is activated by boiling water forced through a stem and returns through a basket of coffee. Refers to someone who is still healthy enough to get around. *"I asked how she was doing, and she said that she is still perkin'."*

Take it with a grain of salt — alludes to a small piece of salt. Refers to a small amount of what is said is truth. *"Take what she says with a grain of salt."*

Can't let go of the apron strings — alludes to the strings of apparel that is worn by someone to protect them from spills and splatters in the kitchen. Refers to someone who is mature but still relies heavily on his/her mother and has not become independent. *"Although she is 21, she has never been able to let go of her mother's apron strings."*

Don't bite the hand that feeds you — may be literal or may be some-one who is providing the food. Refers to advice to someone who is critical or threatening someone who is providing for the person. *"Don't bite the hand that feeds you; he may quit providing for you."*

Eats like a horse — alludes to the large amount of grain a horse eats. Refers to a person who eats large portions or quantity. *"Make plenty of meat and potatoes; he eats like a horse."*

Put on the feed bag — alludes to the bag containing oats that was strapped to a horse's head for more portable and individual feeding. Refers to the readiness of a hearty meal. *"It's time to put on the feed bag."*

Saucered and blewed — alludes to the act of cooling coffee by pouring it from the cup into the saucer and blowing on it. Refers to something that is ready to go or do. *"The job is saucered and blewed."*

Hard to swallow — alludes to the act of taking food into the mouth and having difficulty passing it through the throat. Refers to something that is difficult to believe or accept. *"His rebuke of her is hard to swallow."*

A new broom sweeps clean — alludes to times when the head of a broom was made of bristles from a bunch of shredded sorghum stalks tied together and attached to a stick or wooden handle. The sweeping action soon wears out the bristles. Refers to someone new on a job who does well but will not necessarily continue to work hard. *"Her preliminary evaluation was good, but we all know that a new broom sweeps clean."*

Sweep your own porch first — alludes to broom sweeping the front of the house to create an appropriate appearance. Refers to telling someone that he/she should not be critical of other people before he/she improves his/her own behavior. *"I wouldn't be too critical of him without sweeping your own porch first."*

Swept under the rug — alludes to the rushed action of sweeping the floor dirt under a rug instead of picking it up with a dustpan. Refers to someone hiding information from the public. *"Some important information in the case was swept under the rug."*

Swept him/her off his/her feet — alludes to swishing the broom in sweeping broad strokes. Refers to someone impressing another beyond belief or overwhelming him/her with immediate success. *"He swept her off her feet at the dance."*

Clean sweep — alludes to the process of carefully and completely broom sweeping up dirt into a dustpan. Refers to the successful completion of a series of events or tasks such as in sports. *"They made a clean sweep of the series of games."*

Don't hang your rags on my bush — alludes to airing out cloths used for dusting. Refers to a complaint about blatant and frequent expression and sharing of personal problems. *"Don't hang your rags on my bush; I've got trouble of my own."*

Don't know if she's washin' or hangin' out — alludes to the practice of washing clothes and hanging them outside on a line to dry. Refers to someone who lacks common sense. *"Poor woman, don't know if she's washin' or hangin' out."*

Give her a mirror and a washboard so she can watch herself starve to death — the washboard alludes to the means used by very poor people to wash their clothing. Refers to someone who has married poorly. *"The poor lady, they just as well give her a mirror and a washboard so she can watch herself starve to death."*

Sets a fine table — alludes to someone who prepares good food and presents it well to the guests. Refers to someone who is efficient and effective. *"In preparing for the task, she set a fine table."*

She went after him with a rolling pin — alludes to a heavy, smooth, wooden cylinder with a handle on each end that is used to smooth out dough. Refers to a wife who is very aggressive in her actions.

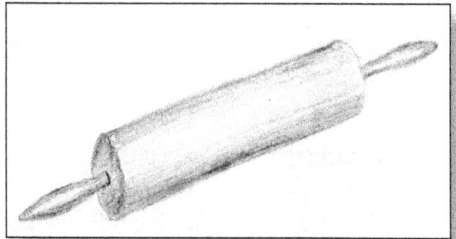

"When he lost their money gambling, she went after him with her rolling pin."

Everything but the kitchen sink — alludes to a small part of the kitchen where the dishes are washed. Refers to an over-exaggeration of all the inclusiveness of a mixture or product. *"She puts everything but the kitchen sink in her stew."*

Sports

Baseball

Got two strikes against 'em — alludes to a batter who has taken two of his allotted three strikes at the balls thrown by the pitcher. Refers to someone who is at a significant disadvantage. *"Jane won't get the promotion; she's already got two strikes against her."*

Right off the bat — alludes to a ball fielded very soon after it was hit. Refers to something that happens quickly such as an action or opinion. *"I liked that guy right off the bat."*

Threw 'em a curve — alludes to a pitcher who throws a ball with unpredictable movement. Refers to unexpected circumstances or behavior. *"She really threw 'em a curve when she said that."*

A pinch hitter — alludes to someone who takes a regular player's place in the batting order. Refers to someone who takes another person's place on short notice. *"She'll be my pinch hitter on this project."*

Went to bat for him — alludes to a player who takes another player's place in the batting order. Refers to someone who supports another or helpfully takes that person's place. *"When I became ill and was criticized by others, she went to bat for me."*

Out in left field — alludes to a player's position or part of the field that doesn't get the action or the number of hit balls that the other positions get. Refers to someone who is out of the action and lacks an awareness of what is going on. (Similar to don't know who's on first base.) *"Don't ask her; she's usually out in left field."*

Call 'em the way you see 'em — alludes to an umpire who calls balls and strikes according to the way he perceives them. Refers to the justification for decision-making processes. *"That's your choice; you have to call 'em the way you see 'em."*

Way off base — alludes to a base runner that takes an extended distance from the established base in order to get a jump on stealing the next base. Refers to someone whose comment or opinion is incongruent with the speaker. *"I agree with you often but on this matter, you are way off base."*

Bush leaguer — alludes to a player who is an amateur or a professional who plays for teams that are located in small remote places. Refers to someone who has not proven his/her ability or merit. *"They shouldn't have promoted her; she's a bush leaguer."*

Out of the ballpark — alludes to a ball that is batted over the ballpark fence for a home run. Refers to something that is far beyond expectations. *"At the auction, the bid on the tractor was out of the ballpark."*

Hum dinger — alludes to a batted ball that travels beyond the ballpark fence for a home run. Refers to something that is exceptional. *"That was a hum dinger of a party and dance."*

Got a lot on the ball — alludes to a pitcher who can throw balls fast and with a lot of action and movement. Refers to someone who is intelligent, dynamic and efficient. *"She's no dummy; she's got a lot on the ball."*

Go for singles, not home runs — alludes to advice to the batters not to try so hard to hit the ball a long distance. Refers to advice to solve minor problems rather than trying to solve everything at once. *"Be patient and take one step at a time; go for singles, not home runs."*

We'll rally in the ninth — alludes to being optimistic with the hope of scoring well in the last inning of the game. Refers to not giving up hope for success is at hand. *"Don't be a pessimist and give up the project; we'll rally in the ninth."*

Got bean balled — alludes to a pitched ball that hits the batter in the head. Refers to a situation in which a person or expressed opinion is discredited by a derogatory remark. *"Every time I make a suggestion, I get bean balled."*

Cleanup batter — alludes to the batter who is scheduled to hit after other hitters are potentially on base. Refers to a person who can culminate transactions for a group. *"In our co-op, she is the cleanup batter."*

Don't drop the ball — alludes to the coach's advice to his fielders. Refers to a manager's advice to personnel in regard to the completion of a transaction or negotiation. *"We've come a long way with this deal; don't drop the ball now."*

Couldn't get to first base — alludes to the description of an inept batter. Refers to the description of a person who is perceived as not being able to even initiate a process or relationship. *"He couldn't get to first base with her."*

Couldn't hit a bull in the butt with a banjo — alludes to a stringed musical instrument with a rather large circular body and the rear end of a male cattle. Refers to someone who lacks physical capabilities, especially a baseball hitter. *"That pinch-hitter couldn't hit a bull in the butt with a banjo."*

You can't get to second unless you take your foot off first — alludes to a coach's advice to a runner in regard to "leading off." Refers to advice to someone who needs to move on in a sequence of action. *"We've discussed the nature of the problem long enough; let's move on to the causes of the problem. You can't get to second unless you take your foot off first."*

Don't get picked off at first — alludes to the advice of the first base coach to the runner to be aware of the pitcher's moves. Refers to a manager's advice to personnel in regard to being cautious when introducing a new concept. *"Beware of the opposing views when introducing this; don't get picked off at first."*

Brought in the big bats or heavy hitters — alludes to the action of
the manager in bringing into the game those who can hit home
runs consistently. Refers to people with the expertise, authority and
credibility to manage or solve problems. *"After the local co-op delayed the
action and negotiation, they brought in the big bats."*

Keep your eye on the ball — alludes to the advice of the batting coach.
Refers to the advice given to a group or discussion participant in
regards to the problem. *"With this group, it's easy to get distracted, but you
have to keep your eye on the ball."*

Check your swing — alludes to a batter who stops his swing at the ball
before it progresses half way and is called a strike. Refers to advice
given to a person who is making an unfavorable comment or
suggestion. *"Check your swing; they appear to know more and different details."*

Take a rain check — alludes to the process of trading your ticket for a
future ticket when the weather prevents the game from being played.
Refers to asking for a future opportunity rather than the current one.
*"Unfortunately, I can't go with you at the scheduled time, but I would like to take
a rain check."*

Struck out — alludes to a batter who has attempted to hit the ball three times
without success. Refers to a failed attempt. *"He struck out with her on their
first date."*

Step up to the plate — alludes to the batter when he is ready for the pitcher
to throw the ball. Refers to requesting that person take a responsibility
or duty. *"Our leader has left us; it is time for you to step up to the plate."*

Card Games

The cards are on the table —
alludes to the time when
the end of the game is near.
Refers to the time in a
process when it is time for
action. *"The cards are on the
table; let's get on with it."*

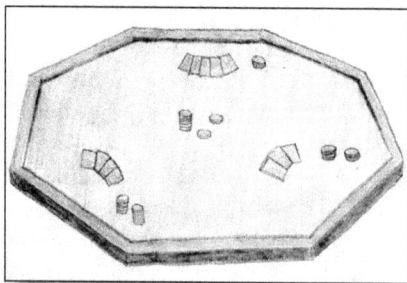

Not playin' with a full deck —
alludes to not having all 52
cards in the deck. Refers to someone who is naïve and lacks common
sense. *"Don't ask him; he's not playin' with a full deck."*

Lost in the shuffle — alludes to losing a card out of the deck while the cards are being mixed and changed in order. Refers to an idea, comment or opinion that gets omitted in a discussion. *"His perspective of the problem got lost in the shuffle."*

Dealing from the bottom of the deck — alludes to taking cards from the bottom of the deck that are placed there intentionally by a slight of hand. Refers to cheating by deception. *"Don't trust him; he'll cheat you by dealing from the bottom of the deck."*

Cut a fair deal — alludes to a player who separates the shuffled cards into two stacks in order to prevent the stacking of the deck by the dealer. Refers to a request to have someone to establish honest and uncorrupted circumstances. *"They cut her a fair deal on the purchase of the car."*

The chips are down — alludes to betting on a card game using token chips. Refers to the necessity of getting on with the procedure or action. *"Let's get going; the chips are down."*

The cards are stacked — alludes to prearranging the cards intentionally to benefit one player. Refers to taking advantage of someone to favor another. *"She won't get the job; the cards are stacked against her."*

According to Hoyle — alludes to an expert, Hoyle, who has published significantly his rules for several card games. Refers to a comment about various rules and procedures. *"According to Hoyle, we should be the first in line."*

Boxing matches as heard on the radio

Down for the count — alludes to a boxer who has been knocked to the canvas and cannot respond before the referee's count to ten. Refers to someone who is no longer in contention for a position or is incapable of succeeding. *"He was down for the count with that company."*

Hit below the belt or a low blow — alludes to an illegal punch that lands below the belt of an opponent. Refers to a scandalous or derogatory comment. *"Her comments and insinuations were hitting below the belt."*

Don't pull any punches — alludes to a fighter's lessening of the intensity of his hits or punches. Refers to expressing oneself without consideration of others' feelings. *"You should tell him how you feel and don't pull any punches."*

Came out swinging — alludes to a boxer as he enters the first round. Refers to a person who begins a discussion or debate with verbal assertiveness. *"When they got to that topic, she came out swinging."*

Knock out — alludes to a punch which knocks the opponent to the canvas and he cannot respond to the referee's count of ten. Refers to a very attractive female whose appearance captivates males. *"His new wife is a real knock out."*

Throw in the towel — alludes to the practice of the trainer throwing a towel in the ring when he believes his fighter is unable to continue to fight. Refers to someone who is ready to quit or give up a project. *"You can tell that she is about ready to throw in the towel with their marriage."*

Stuck between the ropes — alludes to a boxer who is restricted by the ropes of the ring. Refers to someone who is inhibited by the circumstances or situation. *"She really can't retaliate; he has her stuck between the ropes."*

Gave him a black eye — alludes to a boxer who hits his opponent around the eye causing it to bruise and darken. Refers to someone who uses scandalous remarks about someone. *"She gave him a black eye with those remarks."*

Land the first punch — alludes to the advice of the trainer to the boxer. Refers to the advice that one should act immediately and directly. *"In a discussion with her you better land the first punch."*

Rang his bell — alludes to a boxer who knocked his opponents out. Refers to comments that gets one's attention or insults him/her. *"You rang his bell with those comments."*

Got 'em on a TKO — alludes to the referee's stopping a fight when he believes that technically the condition of one of the fighters warrants it. Refers to the stoppage of a procedure or discussion by the leader. *"My project received a TKO before it was fully discussed."*

Give the gift of love, laughter and serious deliberation!

Order extra copies of . . . . .

QUANTITY   **TOTAL**

Listening to Rural Midwestern
Idioms/Folk Sayings $10.95
_____ *Entertaining guide to sayings and expressions*   _____

Other books by Bob Bohlken:

Famous People of Nodaway County $9.95
_____ *Learn about distinguished persons from*
northwest Missouri   _____

Listening to the Mukies and Their
Character Building Adventures $10.95
_____ *Helps kids make good decisions*   _____

Learning to Listen with
Significant Others $14.95
_____ *How listening affects relationships*   _____

SUBTOTAL   _____

MISSOURI RESIDENTS ADD 8.475% TAX _____

SHIPPING
Up to $50...$6.50   **SHIPPING** _____
$51 - $100...$8.75
+ $2 per book thereafter   **TOTAL** _____

My check for $_____ is enclosed.
Please charge my credit card: ❏ Visa ❏ Mastercard

Card #_____ Exp. Date_____

Signature_____

Name_____

Address_____

City_____ State_____ Zip_____

Phone_____ Email_____
Please make check payable to and return to: Images Unlimited Publishing,
P.O. Box 305, Maryville, MO 64468 660-582-4279

Visit us at http://wwwImagesUnlimitedPublishing.com
info@Imagesunlimitedpub.com